"It has been years since I have been so rocked, so moved, by any book, as I have been by *Here After* by the earthquaking new talent Amy Lin. Lin invites us into this place of exquisite pain and beauty; what a great gift she has given us."

—LAUREN GROFF,
author of *Fates and Furies*

"Amy Lin's debut memoir is a testament to everything beautiful and heartbreaking and necessary in this world. With sheer precision and unflinching candor, she shares the depths of love and loss, hope and healing. Not since Joan Didion's *The Year of Magical Thinking* has a book cracked open my heart the way *Here After* has."

—DEBBIE MILLMAN, author of
Why Design Matters and host of *Design Matters*

"How gorgeously *Here After* tackles the twin specters of grief and survival; a steely, symphonic memoir of unexpected loss—and what (necessarily, unbearably) comes next."

—CARMEN MARIA MACHADO,
author of *In the Dream House*

"*Here After* is perfectly titled. Amy Lin's memoir of love and loss is heartbreaking and true. Lin's writing is vivid, episodic, and unflinching—much like grief itself."

—SHANNON LEONE FOWLER,
author of *Traveling With Ghosts*

"*Here After* is a searing account of a young couple's lost future and a writer's descent into the soul-ravaging, shape-shifting wilderness of grief. Amy Lin writes with devastating clarity about the wounds that do not heal, the stories that remain forever fractured, and love's enduring force. This is a profound and essential memoir."

—LAURA VAN DEN BERG,
author of *The Third Hotel*

"Amy Lin knows her way around grief and its constant present tense. Grief is always with us; here are words to go with it, a writer who will accompany you on its long walk. This book made room for my tears and it will make room for yours if you let it."

—MATTHEW SALESSES,
author of *Craft in the Real World*

"As the author navigates the wake of her inexplicable loss, readers will be both humbled by and grateful for the way she brings us into her world. A beautifully visceral and emotionally intimate depiction of young widowhood."

—*KIRKUS REVIEWS* (starred)

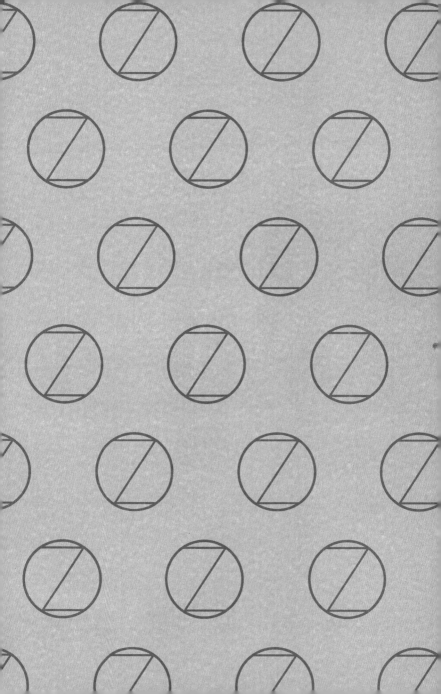

MEET THE AUTHOR

TEASERS,
TRAILERS & MORE...

Here
After

Here
After

Amy Lin

Zibby Books

NEW YORK

Here After: A Memoir
Copyright © 2024 by Amy Lin

All rights reserved. No part of this book may be used,
reproduced, distributed, or transmitted in any form or by any
means without the prior written permission of the publisher,
except as permitted by US copyright law. Published in the
United States by Zibby Books LLC, New York.

Zibby Books, colophon, and associated logos are trademarks
and/or registered trademarks of Zibby Media LLC.

The author has tried to re-create events, locales, and
conversations based on her own memories and those of
others. In some instances, in order to maintain their
anonymity, certain names, characteristics, and locations have
been changed.

"Widowhood and Mortality: A Meta-Analysis and Meta-
Regression," by E. Shor, D. J. Roelfs, M. Curreli, L. Clemow,
M. M. Burg, and J. E. Schwartz, published in *Demography* in
May 2012.

Library of Congress Control Number: 2023946560
ISBN: 978-1-958506-32-5
eBook ISBN: 978-1-958506-33-2

Book design by Neuwirth & Associates
Cover design by Anna Morrison
www.zibbymedia.com

Printed in the United States of America
10 9 8 7 6 5 4 3 2 1

For Kurtis

You pile up associations the way you pile up bricks.
Memory itself is a form of architecture.

—LOUISE BOURGEOIS

The first time I see Kurtis, I do not know who he is.

I am in my car, paused by a pedestrian crosswalk. He passes in front of my vehicle. He is on his way to a blind date. I am on my way to a blind date. He wears a dark blue blazer. His legs are long, his body lithe and graceful.

Why can't I ever meet a man like that? I think. He's gorgeous.

2

Online, a post asks followers:

> What is one thing you wish other people knew about grief?

I read the first twelve of over several hundred responses:

> It doesn't end.
> It won't stop.
> You think about it all the time.
> It never ends.
> It is always with you.
> It doesn't quit.
> It never goes away.
> It is exhausting.
> It is ever present.
> It is always there.
> No amount of time lessens the grief.
> It is forever.

On our first date, June is melting into July. I do not wear a bra. Kurtis tells me he is an architect. I tell him I am a substitute teacher. We both have unusually long hair. His: grazing his shoulders, mine: grazing my hip bones. His father is Japanese, his mother Ukrainian. My father is Chinese, my mother British. We walk through the city. He shows me how the soaring glass panels of the court building make it a gleaming part of the sky. He presses his face to the glass, gazes upward. I have been to court before, contesting a speeding ticket, but I thought nothing of the building. Seeing him love it is how I start to love it myself.

I ride an electric scooter through downtown. It has been just over six years since our first date. Signs of the coronavirus pandemic are everywhere: masks crumpled on the ground, patio tables six feet apart, a hand sanitizer bottle clipped to the scooter's basket. It is August, five months after COVID-19 first shutters doors. Sun gleams from every direction. I make it three blocks on the scooter before a dip in the pavement startles me. I swerve and then I fall, tumbling to the sidewalk. Pain in my left knee leaves me breathless. I text Kurtis and ask him to drive me the rest of the way home.

Of course, Kurtis comes for me. He tries to help me hobble toward the car but I wave him off.

I can do it, I say, hopping on one leg, almost falling.

Kurtis insists I sling an arm around his shoulders. I feel stupid accepting his help. I always feel stupid accepting help.

After our first date, he writes every story I tell him in a note on his phone so he won't forget. I tell my mother he's not boring.

You like him, she says.

She is surprised because I never like anyone.

I do, I say.

6

When we reach home after my spill off the scooter, Kurtis curves gel ice packs around my injured knee every few hours. Still, it swells so much I have an ultrasound to see if I have torn something critical. I celebrate with Kurtis when the lab technician gives me the all-clear.

I got lucky, I say.

At that time, we live in Calgary. We have been married twenty-one months, together almost seven years. Kurtis is thirty-two. I am thirty-one. He brews green tea in glass pots for me and practices magic tricks in our cramped bathroom, which he performs for me later, with relative degrees of success. If he knows it will make me laugh, he vamps naked up and down our small apartment's hallway, twisting his body this way and that, preening for the gleam of my teeth in my mouth as I bare them in a laugh only for him.

I do not always know how to remember.

In certain moments, my life with him feels illusory. A soft sheen falls over our life and it is a delicate thing.

Did it happen?

Was I a wife?

Did he wake up beside me?

Did we laugh?

I know the answers are *yes*, but I know this like I know he is dead—which is to say, none of it feels true all the time.

Would you rather keep your body in perfect health but lose your mind or have your body fall apart but keep your mind?

I ask him this question on our first date, over pints of cider and a plate full of fish tacos.

Body, he says without hesitation.

I am astounded.

That is totally the wrong answer, I say.

When he grins, I see his front teeth are slightly whiter than the rest.

After he dies, I take tests for my family doctor. The first one measures how much my grief affects my life. I score 74.4 percent.

That's really high, my doctor says.

See, I want to say, it really is this bad.

8

Between our first and second date, he finds and reads a blog I wrote during my time overseas at university. When he calls me, he asks why I told him I was a substitute teacher.

You're a writer, he says.

I'm not, I reply.

You are, he says.

I do not know how he can be so sure. I have never even said the words out loud. He is the first.

On our second date, he spends an hour making elaborate grilled cheese sandwiches I cannot eat because of the dairy. He chooses wine I do not like. This all goes in a backpack, alongside a perfectly folded picnic blanket and a portable speaker. He puts me on his spare road bike that is brown and cream.

We set up a hill I cannot handle. I have been sick; my lungs are weak. Also, I am out of shape and he is not. He barrels up the hill so fast—as if it is a flat road. I try to keep up, refusing to admit I cannot. My legs burn. My chest seizes, my breathing shallow. I am dizzy from the exertion. When my front wheel finally inches past his, for a moment I feel like I can do it, but then I am blacking out, plunging off the bike. I come to with his worried face hovering above mine.

After, he tells me it was the worst date ever but I do not agree. I love it. No one has ever gone to so much trouble for me before. No one has ever looked at me so intently, as if everything he did next depended upon me.

Kurtis and I are not at home. We are four hours away, staying with my family in a house near the woods. It is mid-August, two weeks after my fall off the scooter. The next morning, Kurtis and my mother, my father, my sister, and her husband are participating in a "virtual" half-marathon. This means they will be running 21.1 kilometers on the roads around the vacation home.

The half-marathon should have been in person, an official race, with other registered runners, but it is five months into the COVID-19 pandemic and nothing is in person anymore. Racers have been informed that they can run the half-marathon anywhere in Canada—as long as the distance is completed on the specified day. The half-marathon must also be tracked in an exercise app that the race organizers direct runners to download. I cannot run with my family because of my injured knee.

That evening, everyone goes to bed early, resting for the race in the morning. Before Kurtis switches off the light beside the bed, he wraps a blue ice band around my head. I suffer near-daily head-aches that summer, induced by the stress of our upcoming move. He has accepted a job in Vancouver and while it is a dream of mine to live by the ocean, I have never handled change well, even when it is change I want.

I adjust the headband against my temples while he shows me online advertisements for apartments. The pandemic makes flying feel fraught but he thinks we should visit Vancouver soon, to see apartments in person. I am anxious, not just about travel during a pandemic but about leaving Calgary, which means leaving the city I was born in, my family, my teaching job of seven years.

He wants me to write full-time and I have finally agreed to try when we reach Vancouver.

I'm worried, I tell him. *What if I don't write anything at all?*

You're going to write a bestseller, he says.

You can't know that, I say.

He grins, shakes his head at me. We curl together in bed. He switches the subject—asks if I want to hear some *hot goss*.

That night is his last night. The room is entirely dark, light leeched out of it. I am falling asleep. I slip my arm around his leg, set my head on his chest, as always.

Tell me in the morning? I ask, and he says, *Yes.*

Another test I take for my family doctor involves rating my pain on a four-point scale: NONE, MILD, MODERATE, SEVERE.

Here is the list, my doctor says, handing me a sheet of paper.

I start to read the pains a person can experience:

THROBBING

SHOOTING

STABBING

SHARP

CRAMPING

GNAWING

HOT-BURNING

ACHING

HEAVY

TENDER

SPLITTING

TIRING-EXHAUSTING

SICKENING

FEARFUL

PUNISHING-CRUEL

The words swim on the page. I put my finger beside each one and try to focus.

Panic is common, my doctor says. *So is anxiety, sadness, yearning, difficulty concentrating, and confusion about what happens next.*

I pause.

What does happen next? I ask.

12

The first time he tells me he loves me I am not sure I hear right. He has been drinking. His words blur together. We are both naked. In the morning, sober and clothed, he says, *Yes, I mean it.*

I start to hyperventilate, caught in the grip of a panic attack. Whenever I receive something I truly want, I am instantly terrified of losing it. I can find no way in that moment to explain this to him. I cry in gasps, wordless. He is not sure what to do. He leaves, goes out and buys a sesame bagel with vegan cream cheese. We are in New York. Snowflakes cling to the floor-to-ceiling windows of our hotel room. Across the street, I can see the New York Public Library. When he returns, he hovers the bagel in front of my nose while I sob. Eventually, I take a bite. I love him but I am afraid.

I keep trying to warn him. I tell him all the others left. I tell him my intense, my overthink, my chats-a-lot, my never-chats, my aloof. I tell him I do not like television in the morning, or small talk, and I do not clean. I have to choose the music when I am in the car.

I'm not the person for you, I say. *I'll wear you out.*

He nods as if he is agreeing but he is not.

You aren't listening, I say.

I am, he says. *You're just wrong.*

He wakes up early on his final morning. It is August 15, 2020. He hugs me, jostling my still-puffy knee. I cry out in pain, lightly pushing him away. He eats part of a plain bagel and drinks half a yellow sports drink (the worst color, but his favorite).

The running course my family maps out around the house near the woods sees mountains, and hoodoos, large sprays of pines and firs, the gleam of a lake.

He swings his lanky arms back and forth.

I'm a little scared, he says grinning.

He has not run a half-marathon for a few years but he ran track all through university. I know he is not really worried. His limbs are relaxed, his face at ease. Before he walks out of the front door, I say: *Don't go too hard. Love you.*

At the halfway point of the race, my family sees him. They are running toward ten kilometers and he is running away from it, already past kilometer eleven. He is always so much faster than us all. He laughs and claps, cheers for each person by name.

14

You think sadness has a kind of beauty, he tells me once.

I don't, I say but he is right.

He is not right anymore. He is not anything anymore.

Another test for my family doctor, ranking the following phrases on a scale of NEVER, SOMETIMES, OFTEN:

–Most people don't understand how
 severe my condition is

(OFTEN)

–My life will never be the same

(OFTEN)

–No one should have to live this way

(OFTEN)

–I can't believe this happened to me

(OFTEN)

–Nothing will ever make up for all I
  have gone through

(OFTEN)

–I am afraid my condition will
  worsen

(OFTEN)

–I feel like I can't stand it anymore

(OFTEN)

–I can't seem to keep my condition
  out of my mind

(OFTEN)

–There is nothing I can do to reduce
  my symptoms

(OFTEN)

–I wonder whether something
  serious may happen

(*Something serious is happening*, I tell my family
doctor)

–My symptoms are awful and I feel
  they overwhelm me

(OFTEN)

–I worry all the time about whether
  my symptoms will end

(OFTEN)

He does not come back through the door but my father does.

Get in the car, he says. *It's Kurtis.*

Sweat flattens my father's salt-and-pepper hair against his forehead. I am wearing black shorts and an oversized pale pink crewneck sweatshirt.

My father drives less than one kilometer to a pedestrian bridge beside the highway. The drive takes under a minute. The bridge is a silver grid, open to the river beneath. I pray out loud in the car. It is the first time I have prayed in years.

On the bridge: an ambulance, people, traffic stopped in both directions. I start toward the ambulance but an RCMP officer halts me. He asks who I am.

I'm the wife, I say.

I ask how long he has been unconscious. The police officer looks behind his shoulder without answering. We watch the violent up and down motions of a paramedic performing CPR. My heart beats steadily. No panic, no terror, no fear.

Years ago, a cyclist strikes my mother from behind while she and I are running together. She is unconscious on the ground for several minutes. Blood weeps from her striped headband, turns her short pale brown hair dark. I am so calm both the emergency responder and the emergency room doctor tell me I am *good in a crisis*. I thank them, my clothes covered in her blood.

16

In the summer, we walk to Amato Gelato and order double-scoop waffle cones. He loves ice cream. Dairy burns inside my intolerant gut but the ritual is so sweet. I order the same thing every time—mocha chocolate brownie—and Kurtis dithers, wanting to try something new, overwhelmed by choice. One time, he orders one of his favorites, mint chocolate, and the young guy scooping says: *Man, there are a lot of things to live for but this flavor ain't it.*

He can never make decisions without asking for my opinion. He asks me which boxer briefs to wear in the morning, which lunch to buy while he is at work, which blazer goes with his pants (and do I like the pants?). I ask him, when we are engaged, how someone so indecisive can be so sure I am the one for him.

You weren't a choice, he says. *It was always you.*

17

Before I climb back into the car to follow the ambulance taking Kurtis away, I see my sister. She is sitting on a patch of grass near the bridge. Her whole body shakes.

I am trying to be brave, she tells me.

Her teeth clatter against one another.

It's going to be okay, I say, though neither she nor I believe it.

On the way to the hospital, I ask my father the question the officer refused to answer directly.

How long?

A long time, my father says.

He looks at me without turning his head.

I know the stats, I say.

At least once a week, sometimes more if I have not slept or we have been apart recently, I ask Kurtis: *Are you going to leave me?*

In the hospital, my father and I sit in a small room filled by a hulking machine. He sits perfectly still, his large hands resting on his bony knees. When the doctor joins us, I am struck by the blue of her surgical mask, which matches her eyes perfectly. She tells my father and me everything that has been done: CPR, defibrillation, other actions I lose because the words are rising in my throat, coming out of my mouth, interrupting her.

My husband is dead, I say.

She nods. Yes, they called the code. Asystole for over an hour. His heart never regained any kind of rhythm.

The doctor and my father leave me alone then, at my request. I stare at the machine and wonder what it is. I cannot comprehend its massive shape, cannot understand how something so large fits in a room so small. My body feels numb.

Everything seems impossible. I touch my nose, my lips, my chin, to see if it is all still there. My brain catalogues the room: grey walls, grey machine, greyish white tile. Grey green chair covers. Taupe bandage on my knee, tied poorly and too loosely.

After my mother is hit by the cyclist, she recovers fully and more quickly than the doctors expect. She has no memory of the accident, but I am haunted by recurring nightmares of my mother's slack face pressed to the pavement. RJ, my therapist, tells me the nightmares stem from the horror I repressed in order to stay calm while my mother was bleeding on the ground.

You won't let yourself experience your fear, RJ says.

That's our way, I say.

My mother could only whisper it. Hazel eyes wide, delirious, strapped to the stretcher, she breathes it in my ear: *I'm a little afraid,* she says. *I'm a little. I'm.*

I leave the small hospital room because the police need me to officially identify him.

I can do it, my father offers but I shake my head.

I limp into the emergency department. The doctor directs me to a small room on my left.

He is stretched out on the yellow spinal board the emergency responders used to transport his body from the bridge to the hospital. The board rests on top of an examination table. The doctor tells me I can touch him through the sheet draped over his midsection. I assume this is to conceal the damage the CPR and other emergency procedures have done to his body.

I first see the soles of his running shoes that never fit properly, giving him massive blisters. Then, his eyes: open, brown and big, as they were in life, but death blows them out larger, lightens the brown, turns them glassy.

At the roots, his hair crusts white with sweat. He is so still. His skin looks set, the way milk does when it is heated. There is a mild abrasion in the middle of his forehead. The scrape is brown. Through the sheet, I can see the slight curve where his hands are resting. I touch the top of his right hand through the fabric. I tell him I love him.

His autopsy takes more than eight months. The report shows his physical form is in perfect condition. His heart, his brain, his other vital organs, all healthy, without any discernable defects. There is no known or visible reason for him to be dead, except that he is.

21

When he dies, I fall out of time.

22

The call I place to my husband's parents is recorded. I do not realize this until later, pushing PLAY on a new voice mail only to hear my wavering voice telling my husband's parents to *pull over*. They are driving. Their phone, which wirelessly connects to their car speaker, records the call and sends it to me. I relive my husband's father's scream and then my husband's mother's. I hear my voice saying I am sorry, but I can't tell them if they are screaming.

I cannot listen to the rest of the recording. I save it, though I do not know why. Then, I call others: his siblings; his best friends; his boss; my boss. I text my close friends.

He's gone, I write.

Later, I realize my two-word message is cryptic but in the moment it feels so obvious to me that I am communicating he died. Kurtis died.

23

After our wedding, he frames our vows, sets them side by side on the dresser. He places all the cards we received on our dresser too, even laying the Polaroids we took around the cards. Sometimes, I find him sitting on our bed, admiring his handiwork. Other times, I catch him photographing his left hand, his ring finger encircled by his wedding band, which he never takes off.

I love being your husband, he tells me.

Before I leave the hospital on the day of Kurtis's death, my father hands me a tissue. When the folds relax, they unveil Kurtis's wedding ring. I am in awe of my father's presence of mind. I slide the ring onto the middle finger of my left hand, where it fits a little loosely. A cry ripples from my throat. I bend forward. My father strokes my back while my tears drip onto white tile. This is the first time I cry.

24

I meet my therapist, RJ, when I am twenty-five. RJ takes notes on a lined pad of yellow paper. He has merry eyes and laughs in such a forthright way that at first it surprises me and then it relaxes me.

In my midtwenties, I am vegan and my dyed blond hair is so long that even when it is braided, it reaches my belly button. I only wear black. I think I cannot feel anything good. I believe, steadfastly, I am not lovable. This makes my longing to meet someone particularly painful.

Help me love somebody, I say to RJ in our first session.

Have you met anyone recently? he asks.

I have a blind date next week, I say. *A guy named Kurtis, with a K.*

The day Kurtis dies, I send RJ a one-line email telling him what has happened. RJ calls me immediately.

Do not grieve alone, he says because he knows me.

25

When my father and I return to the house near the woods, I stay outside. I try to limp to the bridge where Kurtis was found, but it is too hot. I am still in the pink sweatshirt and it is sweltering outside. I collapse beneath the shade of towering evergreens. I try to talk to him, but I cannot. Heat shimmers on the pavement. I hear a faint rustle but when I poke about in the bushes, nothing is there. My body feels made of concrete. I sit there for hours, though it does not feel like it.

Eventually one of my best friends, Brayden, finds me. We have been close for almost ten years. Light flares brassy on his curly hair, which is bright red and grown long because pandemic regulations have shut down hair salons and barbershops.

I had texted Brayden from the hospital and asked him to come get me. As he approaches, I see he is wearing a white T-shirt and brown leather sandals. His thick hair is still wet from the shower. He has driven hours. The house near the woods is not even in the same province as Calgary. I reach up from the ground and hug his midsection.

What am I going to do now? I ask.

If Kurtis or I climb out of bed at an odd hour, the other stirs.

Don't worry, we whisper to each other. *Just going to the bathroom. Everything is okay.*

26

I am always watching Kurtis. He catches me staring the night before he dies. I take him in: the pink skin blemish beside his mouth, the crinkles beside his eyes, the flat bounce of his ass. Upon seeing me see him, his smile cracks open something so handsome and light in him that in turn it cracks open something in me. His joy is so painful, so true, even after all our years, I am still unprepared for the abundant wave that passes through my body.

He's here, I think with the same feeling of wonder as when I first met him.

It is probably not feminist to say, I say to RJ, *but when he loved me, everything in my life got better.*

Neither Brayden nor I can stand music in the car. He talks, I listen.

Tell me something else, I say if he stops speaking.

Brayden drives exactly the speed limit; his hands set on the wheel at a perfect ten and two. My parents are an hour behind us. I am afraid if my mother and father and I get into the same vehicle, the magnitude of our collective grief will drive us off the road.

In Brayden's apartment, I scream-sob into one of his pillows. At one point, Brayden reaches out to steady my shaking shoulders. I startle. It is such steady warmth. I grip his hand. I do not let go until my mother texts and says they are home. I live in their guest bedroom for the next fourteen months. My mother sleeps in the same bed as me for at least two.

28

On Sundays, Kurtis and I sit in our pajamas on our couch. We talk about things like vitality and truth and regret while we eat thick-crust sourdough toast. The bread is sprinkled with pink salt and black pepper, skinned with golden butter. Sometimes, I get so into what we are talking about that I cannot stop my stream of words. He grins, listening.

I know, I say when I finally take a breath, *I talk too much.*

He shakes his head.

No, baber, he says. *Not even close.*

He favors a variant of the word "babe" I have never heard until I meet him. The *no* comes out with a little puff of incredulous air.

After Kurtis dies, I email a woman named Rebecca. I only know two things about her. The first: she attended the same university I did. The second: her husband is dead.

Kurtis is still alive when I initially learn of Rebecca's loss through social media; someone I follow shares a link to Rebecca's husband's obituary.

Listen, I say.

Kurtis and I are sitting together on the couch. I read the obituary aloud.

This is like if you died this year, I say when I am finished reading. I look at Kurtis. *He's the same age as you. This is like if you died.*

My chest squeezes with panic saying the words.

Don't, Kurtis says, tears coming to his eyes. *I'm right here. We're right here. That's not our story.*

It is March, days before the World Health Organization declares COVID-19 a pandemic. I ask Kurtis if I should contact Rebecca and offer condolences. Neither of us is sure. I decide not to reach out because I do not really know her. I do not want to intrude. I have yet to realize silence only isolates the bereaved even more than death already has.

When I tell RJ I have messaged Rebecca, he nods.

It could help, he says. *Connecting with another widow.*

Nothing helps, I say.

We are talking because he has called me every day since Kurtis died and not charged me a single cent.

He might have had time to think, 'I'm going to pass out,' the coroner, a woman named Susan, tells me. *Or he might have felt woozy, but then he would have been gone.*

She informs me based upon the pattern of injuries on his body, it is inarguable that he was dead by the time his body struck the bridge.

Days after he dies, I allow the RCMP officer to share my phone number with the young woman who first found Kurtis on the bridge. She is the one who called 911.

Almost instantaneous, I tell the young woman.

She is worried he was alive when she happened upon him. She talks to me for over an hour.

There was nothing more you could have done.

It is what she wants to hear but it is also true.

I read on the internet that the auditory sense is often the last to go. I like to believe this means he heard the water as he went, heard the river running below him, water that is still running now, even though he is no longer.

31

I tell Brayden I have made a sport of searching "bridges near me" on the internet. He shakes his head.

Amy, he says dryly, *there aren't any bridges in this city high enough for that.*

There isn't anything else to say. It's gallows humor but that's us. Brayden is an intensive care nurse. He is seeing so many people dying on ventilators in the ICU every day. I am ignoring the search engine's suggestion that I call a helpline.

I read online that another young widow has a sister who texts her each morning. The sister asks the widow to rate her day on a scale of one to ten. Ten means her husband has returned. One means the safety is off. If the widow texts her sister and the number is at or below a three, her sister comes over after work.

Upon reading this, I begin to check on myself. Most days, I land at a four, wavering toward a three.

RJ tells me days like the four and the three are essential to living, though they seem to threaten existence. He says when I feel that way, I must open up.

Ideally, he says, *open up to someone you trust. Cry in front of them. Tell them your pain.*

I think about myself as a child: terrified of crying in front of others. Afraid of being overwhelmed by my sadness.

I am never going to do that, I say.

No one heals in isolation, he tells me. *You have to reach out. You cannot survive this alone.*

I don't want to survive, I say.

32

During our honeymoon in Japan, I climb the stairs of our ryokan and find him in the scalding water of the rooftop patio's onsen. Around us, trees heavy with foliage close in. The sound of a nearby waterfall is the only voice, other than ours. He grins at me. Steam glazes his skin. I bask in him all over again—his huge brown eyes, his quick, fine fingers, his mane of gorgeous hair. His nail beds are shell pink. He has brought nothing with him, no book or music or phone. It is just him and me and the water and the dark green mountain.

This is our life, he says looking directly at me, sweat at his brow like a diadem. *This is it*.

Understand: I have never known how to love something in moderation.

The afternoon I meet Rebecca it is autumn. The day before, leaves were green but now they fall into yellow piles at my feet. It always happens like that.

Rebecca has short red-gold hair I admire while we sip cups of tea. She is only a year older than I am. We are sitting outside on her apartment's patio. I tell her I think Kurtis would have resisted the spiritual passing, if there is one.

He would not have gone quietly, I say. *Not without me.*

After all, he used to text me from the bathroom if it was a particularly long visit.

Rebecca and I talk about this ghost limb, this love, we have for our beloveds. We keep wondering if they are cold or if they need rest or what they might like for dinner.

I tell Rebecca most nights, when he came home from work, I would ask: *Did you eat today?*

He would smile, his eyes going big, like a small kid caught out. I would say his name in the way I did when I was upset but only for show.

You have to eat! I would say.

He would tell me he knew. He tended to skip meals when he was busy or stressed. Often, I would text him at lunch, to make sure he ate. I explain to Rebecca that I find myself picking up my phone around noon before I realize thoughts like these, thoughts about what he needs, now have no use. I ask Rebecca if she thinks our loved ones—if there is an After and they are in it—can hear us when we call for them?

Of course, there is no answer to my question. There is no way to know. Rebecca has different questions too. Questions to which I do not have any answers. Neither of us has to explain the pain we are in to the other. That is something at least.

A month after I meet Kurtis on our blind date, I sign my first full-time teaching contract. It is the beginning of my career as an elementary school educator. Three months after this, in January, I begin a master's degree in creative writing.

I work all the time. It is work I want to do but it overwhelms me. I cry a lot. Almost every night of the week for years, until I finish my degree, and teaching begins to feel like a job I know how to do, he makes me dinner, hands me tissues for my nose when I am bawling, tells me, *Baber, you're not*, even when I am saying, *I know I am. I know I'm crazy.*

On our honeymoon in Tokyo, it is much colder than we expected. My tears start halfway up a mountain.

I wanted to go to Cuba, I wail while other tourists inch away from him and me.

It's just a little farther, he says.

I want to quit but I follow him anyway.

Just a bit more, he says. *That's it. You can.*

When I am in it, love can make me believe anything.

After spending time with Rebecca, I do not go home. Instead, I drive to a plaza at the edge of the city center. I sit in my car in the parking lot and sob.

Kurtis worked on the plaza. He takes me there when we are barely dating. He shows me a large art installation made of multiple vertical aluminum fins—all the silver blades stand in a curved row. The fins glow with white lights when the train rushes by the plaza. I love the design, but even more, I love the way the lights move across his face. He is illuminated in ways I have not seen before.

The plaza remains. Every day people walk through it, sit in it, look at it. Every day, people experience this part of Kurtis that is metal and wood and light. This does not bring me the comfort people seem to think it will.

What is it called? I ask when he first shows the plaza to me.

Celebration Square, he says. *But everyone just calls it C-Square.*

I do not remember what we did after. I do not remember leaving. I just remember sitting there beside him, watching for a train that was supposed to come.

What is the difference between a graveyard and a cemetery?

This is one of the things I wonder the day my family and I tour the grounds of the place we ultimately choose for his memorial bench. As we are assessing one area's potential, I say to my father: *It would be easier to think without all this goddamn noise.*

The noise is a high-pitched buzzing from which there is no break or escape.

They're engraving someone's headstone, my father says. He gestures down the hill toward the men crouched near the epicenter of the sound.

Oh God, I say, understanding he is right.

We look at each other and I laugh, though it is more a hoarse bark then anything else. The action sends pain through my chest. I grab my ribs. They have been painful for days.

All the crying must have strained something, I assume.

I stagger over the small hills of beautifully maintained grounds. There is also a pain in my left groin that radiates into my inner thigh.

My leg feels wooden, I say.

It's a little discolored, my mother says.

Is it?

We look more closely, but cannot be sure.

Kurtis and I are not always happy. We have a particularly difficult season.

You have a version of me in your head, I say. *But you don't know me.*

It is hard for me to admit this because I feel how much he loves me. Yet you can love someone in this capacious way and still fail to really see them. I was trying to tell him that. I was trying to tell him there was the person he thought me to be and there was the person I knew myself to be. Most of the time, I wanted to try to be the woman he believed I was, but I was not really her. He and I cry together.

You don't know the names of my pains, I say.

I'll learn, he says.

Two months after he dies, I take to searching variants of "young widows" online. One afternoon, my search yields a meta-analysis on widowhood and mortality. In the report, I read that statistically, the widowed are two and a half times more at risk of dying by suicide in the first year of widowhood. The report also informs me I am twenty-two percent more likely than the married to die of other causes such as cerebral or cardiac events, cancer, or car crashes. These illnesses and incidents may seem random but are, in fact, not.

The study emphasizes that this increased susceptibility is most notable in "younger" widows, a group defined as those in their forties and fifties.

Those widowed in their thirties, such as myself, are also more prone to these causes of death than their married peers, but there are just too few people widowed in this age group to collect measurable data.

This is all a way of saying that being widowed young literally puts one's life at higher risk. This increased vulnerability is termed the widowhood effect.

39

After touring the cemetery, my father, who is a doctor, looks at my leg that my mother and I think might be discolored. I show him where it hurts, near my groin. He insists that he and my mother take me to the hospital emergency room. He thinks I have blood clots in the veins of my leg.

At the hospital, when my father tells this theory about clots to the nurse, her eyebrows arch in surprise. Most people presenting with deep vein thrombosis—this is the technical name for a blood clot—are over forty years old. While we wait for a doctor to see me, I run my hands along my left calf. The skin is stretched tight, the flesh swollen. I massage my left, aching thigh in slow, smooth circles.

I can't have a deep vein thrombosis, I reason. My husband just died ten days ago.

Surely, I think, that is enough.

We start attending therapy together. Kurtis learns my pains. Sometimes, he so accurately identifies why I feel a certain way that I pretend to gasp.

How dare you? I say, grinning.

He dissolves into laughter brought about from the joy of discovery.

On the phone, I overhear him talking to his best friends. He tells them to go to counselling.

It's a game changer, he says.

I listen and marvel at his capacity to love. It makes him so unafraid of change. He takes it all as a matter of course. He forgives everything.

This is not an exaggeration because he is dead. He really was like that.

41

A month after Kurtis dies, RJ says if I will not open up to a safe person and tell them about my grief, then maybe I can write down how I am feeling and share it with someone instead. I do not refuse the writing, but I refuse the sharing.

It is too much for one person, I say.

The last trip we take is for our first wedding anniversary. It is November. Calgary at that time of year is a frigid minus twenty degrees Celsius and snowing. When it is that cold, I step outside and my nose hairs freeze together in my nostrils.

We fly to Bermuda in the middle of the night. When we arrive, it is so warm we stand outside in the pitch dark and listen to tree frogs scream. After a moment, we tuck our suitcases inside the apartment. Then, we leave. It is late but we are determined to see the ocean.

The roads in Bermuda are narrow, without sidewalks or lights, but he has thought of this. He wears a red, blinking safety light on his belt loop and straps a blue headlamp to his head. I navigate via a map on my phone. When we reach the beach, the surf is loud and water foams at our toes, warmer than we expect. As sand shifts beneath our sandals, we feed airplane pretzels to little, fat brown birds that hop up to us, peering at us through keen eyes.

Eventually, we wend our way back to the apartment. We go single file—him, the light ahead, me following, calling out directions.

At the hospital, I am sent for an ultrasound. The woman performing it has a young, soothing voice. She spreads cool gel down my left leg from my groin to my knee. The round plastic ball of the transducer presses against my flesh and the room fills with the clicking sounds of the Doppler. I flinch when she reaches the flesh near my knee, which is still tender from the fall off the scooter. When she finishes scanning my leg, she tells me she is going to look at the veins in my abdominal cavity—the space in the body that holds organs like the intestines. I wonder why.

Isn't the clot supposed to be in my leg?

I'm just being thorough, she says.

This is something that sounds good but in fact generally means something on the screen has prompted a sudden intensity of focus, a renewed commitment to *being thorough.*

I stare at the blank ceiling tiles and wonder when Kurtis will call me. I have so much to tell him.

44

The ultrasound shows I have large clots in the femoral vein of my left leg. I also have clots in the veins of my abdominal cavity and in my lungs. The ER doctor on call who tells me all this asks if I have had rib pain or trouble breathing recently. I say, *Yes . . . but grief. Yes . . . but all the crying.*

Yes, he says, *clots.*

He tells me I am going for a CT scan. This will help the doctors get a better understanding of how far into my chest the clots extend. It is serious, what is happening to me.

Have you had a CT before? the technician asks.

I shake my head. She tells me to be very still, that when the scan begins, I will feel warmth in my groin, like I have urinated.

Don't trust the feeling, the technician says. *You won't have peed yourself.*

On the ceiling tiles, someone has painted big, awkward butterflies.

Don't trust the feeling, I think.

I stare at the winged insects. The primary-colored paint is cracked and peeling. I have a feeling my husband is dead.

In Tokyo, we visit the Sensoji temple and its markets. The corridors are so packed with people that he and I walk one in front of each other. When we find the stall where we can draw fortune papers from a wooden box, we do. His is bad, so he lets it go. Mine is good, so I keep it.

He draws only bad fortunes the whole trip but we think barely anything of this. He throws his fortunes into garbage bins. I fold mine, bending the almost-translucent slips of paper in half, sliding them into his pockets for him to hold.

While hospitalized, part of my brain is screaming: *Your life is at risk!* This part of my brain is telling me to do what I can to live. Yet, another part of my brain is telling me to stop trying to live. This part has been telling me to die ever since Kurtis did.

It has only been ten days, I think. If I go now, I can still find him. He might even be waiting for me.

I am especially concerned if there is an After, Kurtis will be lost in it, or confused, perhaps even unsure. He could be like that if he did not have time to prepare. Mostly, though, I do not want him to be alone. He always wanted us to be together. He would tell me all the time.

One sticky summer evening, I am downing whiskey gingers in a bar named Starlite. I text Kurtis from the dance floor, tell him to join me. The night before, we watched our first movie together. He called it a *film*. It was our third date. As the credits rolled, he turned to me, grinning as widely as I had ever seen, and said, *This is the best! I'm so glad you're here.*

By the time I message Kurtis from the bar, it is so late. He should have been sleeping. Still, he enters the bar dancing, his hands and legs jiving in a full-body hallelujah. We sway to the beat together while go-go dancers in gold sequin miniskirts twist on a raised platform above us. Then, the bar closes.

Was it worth it? I ask, spilling out onto the street. *Making it for just one song?*

He pushes his dark hair back from his face.

Oh, he says, *absolutely.*

After the CT scan, I am officially admitted into the hospital. A white identification bracelet is clasped around my left wrist. IV bags are hung on thin silver poles and put on a drip into my body. In one bag: Heparin, a blood thinner. In the other: TPA, which a vascular surgeon explains is like Draino, but for veins.

A real clot buster, he says.

The drugs aren't enough, the surgeon emphasizes. He wants me to undergo something called an AngioJet thrombectomy.

I have questions. He has answers.

Yes, it is an aggressive approach.

Yes, it essentially involves threading a tube into my left leg's vein and vacuuming out as many clots as possible.

No, I will not be entirely unconscious. I will be sedated, partially conscious.

It is this way so I can report any searing head pain (stroke), chest pain (heart attack), or difficulty breathing (lung collapse).

He tells me he requires my consent to proceed.

If you don't agree, he says, and then shrugs.

Mortality rates are not good for clots as severe as mine.

I decide to take RJ's advice about writing because I do not know what else to do. I am overcome by what feels like limitless sorrow. I tell RJ I will write a letter about how I feel each week. I will make the posts public, for anyone to read. I show him the website I will use.

It's like a digital newsletter, I tell him.

I explain that people can access the letters when or if they want to read them. This way, one person alone does not have to feel obligated to help me bear the enormity of my grief.

Are you sure? RJ asks me.

He is worried someone as private as I am will struggle with something as public as what I have suggested.

No, I say. *I am not sure.*

49

I agree to the AngioJet because I do not know that I believe in an After and also if I die, my parents will scream the way his parents did.

Before the Angio, there is a COVID-19 nasal test and a catheter, which the nurse holds up in front of me. I look at the plastic bag, the long, yellowed tube.

It's not so bad, my mother says, answering my facial expression.

Your urethra was easy to find! the nurse exclaims once the catheter is in.

I like her joy, but I cannot find mine.

At my insistence, he buys products for his face. The first time he exfoliates and moisturizes, he acts as if he has invented skin care. Turning his face this way and that, he lets it catch the light, asks me if it is shining.

I feel radiant, he says.

He was always turned toward delight. Without him, I am not sure what axis I am on, if I can turn at all.

In radiology, where the AngioJet procedure is done, I look at the ceiling, my breath warm behind my mask. I am afraid, though I do not know of what.

A woman with white-blond hair tells me they are starting the sedative. She says I will feel drowsy soon, but I will not be entirely unconscious. The Heparin and TPA continue to drip into my body. It is unusual, I learn later, to run both drugs at the same time. It is a sign of the severity of my situation. When the nurse checks on me again, I am not drowsy.

You're going to need a bigger gun, I say.

I wonder if Kurtis has eaten while I am waiting for the sedative to kick in. Again, I have to remind myself he is no longer a body that needs sustaining. I am weary, tired of falling into thoughts that are for him, thoughts for which there is no longer any necessity.

Then, a tearing, hot sensation along my left leg, above my knee.

Is that the AngioJet? I ask.

From somewhere a reply: *Yes, that's the AngioJet.*

One of my best friends, Selene, writes every morning at eleven. When I tell her about the letters I am starting to write about my grief, she tells me I can join her each morning via video call, so I do not have to work alone.

Most days, we do not speak. Selene ties her dark hair up off her neck and lights a candle. Sometimes, she turns her computer screen so I can see the froth of palm fronds outside her window.

When I cannot hide that I am crying, my sniffing amplified by the microphone, Selene asks if I want to talk about it. If I do, she does not tell me to stop. She just sits with me, on the other end of the line, and allows my pain to exist.

52

Sometimes, Kurtis and I fight so late into the night the only take-out still available by the time we resolve our issues is fast-food chicken strips and pizza. We haggle over which to order—me preferring the former, him the latter. Regardless of what we choose, we stay up even later and eat together, fresh in that raw tenderness following a fight.

After the Angio finishes, I am sent to the intensive care unit to lie flat on my back. I must be entirely still for twenty-four hours. This allows the blood thinners to reach the clots that the Angio could not remove. I am woken every hour for vitals checks and blood draws, which are used to monitor the level of medication in my body. The nurse uses a handheld Doppler to hear the pulse in both my feet. I am asked every hour if I have head pain, or chest pain, while the nurse flashes a penlight at my pupils. Almost as frequent as the checks are the moments when I vomit. I throw up so much stomach acid that thick, stinking fluid covers my gown.

After twelve hours in the ICU, my back muscles seize. I am in terrible pain I cannot alleviate as I am not yet allowed to move.

After twenty-four hours, the vascular surgeon visits me. He tells me the thinners have done *good work, but . . .*

My head lifts off the hospital pillow.

But . . .

He thinks it would be best if I undergo one more AngioJet. Higher in my chest, the clots in a vein named the inferior vena cava have not dissolved as much as he had hoped.

No, I say. *It is all so painful. I am so tired.*

It would be better, the doctor says, *in the long run.*

My husband died at thirty-two, I say. *Do not tell me about "the long run."*

The fights Kurtis and I have can be so drawn out it seems as if they will never end. At the time, I think these fights are some of the worst feelings I will ever experience.

53

Kurtis is drunk. We are at a wedding. It is the small hours of the morning. Everyone who is not in their twenties or thirties has gone home. Late-night snacks—fried chicken and spring rolls—have been served. Kurtis and I are seated at a long rectangular table around which most of his friends are seated too. All of them are still drinking.

At the head of the table, one of Kurtis's friends has unbuttoned his shirt so he can rub two fried chicken drumsticks against his bare chest.

Society will tell me it's wrong, he slurs. *But it feels so right.*

Kurtis laughs, slumped against my body. Grease turns the guy's skin shiny. Kurtis is considering joining the drumstick activity. I tell him it might be time to drink some water.

If you don't hydrate now, I say, *you will puke all night.*

He tells me he never pukes, which we both know is a lie.

I walk him to the bar and he promises me he will get water. Then, he orders four vodka waters. The drinks arrive on a brown circular tray.

Don't do it, I say.

He stares at me. I am trying not to laugh. Without breaking eye contact, he picks up the first vodka water and drains it. I start to laugh, because how can I not?

Refreshing, he says.

He has the audacity to wink while I shake my head.

54

After the second AngioJet, one of the nurses, a woman wearing duck-patterned scrubs, asks me: *Do you want to see your clots?*

I sit up slightly in my hospital bed. She shows me a large, glass jar with a tightly sealed lid. Floating in clear liquid is a web of thin red strings, from which hang dark red blood clots of varying sizes, like strange, fleshy pearls. They are so much smaller than I expect.

At the funeral home, the director explains the contents of an oversized stack of paper. I sign multiple times for things I only barely understand. The director says something about the federal government. He hands me a pen, which he notes is *clean*—another strange tic of dealing with a death amid a global pandemic. I sign and sign. I have no idea what I am agreeing to but my parents are with me and they support my signing.

When we finish, the director takes us down the hallway and opens a dark wood door. Caskets fill the room. One corner is dedicated to urns.

No, I say, but too quietly for anyone to hear.

My family mills around the room, pointing to possible casket options. I cannot make sense of it all. Why does he need a casket? He is being cremated. My parents explain the casket is burned with the body. My mother asks what I want engraved on the urn. Woozy, I lean against the wall near the door. Every choice buckles my mind.

56

Flowers keep coming for me.

Bouquets fill the entire surface of my parents' dining room table. I lie on my parents' couch and stare at the blossoms for hours.

Kurtis always keeps me in flowers too. Once, a massive arrangement of white roses arrives on the doorstep. It is a celebratory time for me; I am graduating from my master's program. I open the door and find the blooms, their petals fleshy and soft to the touch, like skin.

These are unbelievable! I say.

There are so many roses, perfectly held together by ivory ribbon.

I thought you would like them, he says.

I pull out the card tucked between the rose heads.

Congratulations, I read out loud. *Love, Mum and Dad*.

I look up. Kurtis has gone uncharacteristically pink.

Oh my God, he says.

Did you just take credit for flowers that aren't yours? I ask.

I have to set the vase down on the carpet I am laughing so hard.

I am so embarrassed, he says. *Never tell your parents.*

When Kurtis's white roses arrive, the arrangement is so much smaller than my parents' that he just lies on the carpet, face down, theatrically groaning.

The day I take my body to see his body at the funeral home I choose to enter the room alone. I have been released from the hospital only a few days prior. I am weak and I have to use a walker to support myself as I move around. When I push open the mahogany doors of the viewing room and hobble into the room, the casket is much farther from the door than I thought. I can only make out the slight puff of his hair across the distance. Fear runs through me. I cannot move or speak. I am afraid if I do, he will wake up. He would be scared, too—trapped in a casket, coming to consciousness. How would I explain everything?

I pull a chair about ten feet from the casket. From where I am sitting, I can see part of his nose and his cheeks, the pale mound of his hands folded over his stomach. I inch the chair closer. I say his name out loud—quietly. When nothing happens, I say his name loudly, almost a shout. He does not move. I pull the chair in farther. I am maybe two or three feet away from him then. I tell him it is time for him to come back. I tell him I need him to return my calls. I tell him I cannot do any of it without him. Still, he makes no movement. So, I stand up and close the last stretch of distance between us.

His suit does not look quite right. I realize his body has bloated and the tailored jacket no longer fits properly. It is the suit he wore for our wedding. I look at his hair next. Whoever prepared him for the viewing did his hair perfectly. It is exactly like his hair when he was alive. I reach out and fear flares: What if it is not his hair anymore?

My fingers land on the strands. The fear sinks down. This is his hair: silky, thick. The beds of his fingernails are blue, completely unlike their normal shade. His eyes are closed this time; his face looks older than I have ever seen it. There is a bulge of flesh behind his ears that is exactly as it was in life.

You are so beautiful, I say.

58

We go to Flamenco Fest. It is packed with people, loud with the sounds of mediocre guitarists and steamy with the scent of overpriced food. I want to leave immediately. Still, we stay. He is always so convinced things will get better.

At this festival he tells me he was wait-listed when he applied for architecture school. Instead of just seeing what would happen, he called and asked the registrar how he could improve his application. The registrar put him in touch with a few professors in the program—for advice—but they never replied to his emails. So, he kept calling the registrar. He tells me he phoned so much, eventually, the program accepted him.

Your persistence! I say in admiration.

He laughs as he tells me all this, his head bobbing in perfect time to the music.

How are you?

They keep asking me. Friends, acquaintances, strangers: they all say these things to me.

How are you doing?

I do not know how to reply.
He's dead, I say.
They wince.
Passed away, they say.

I stop answering.

Oh, you know, I say.

I'm doing, I say.

60

After his hair, I touch his shoulder and find it rigid. It is so unlike him—he was so warm and soft—that I pull my hand back quickly, do not touch that part of his body again. The scratch in the center of his forehead is flawlessly covered. I can barely make it out, and only because I am looking for it.

Somewhere outside the room, someone turns on music that blares through the speakers. I text my parents who are waiting for me outside the room—I cannot drive with my injured leg and the medications I am taking. Even though I wanted to see Kurtis alone, I am grateful my parents are with me. I ask them to see if the music can be turned off. In a minute, the room falls silent again.

I tell him the things I have been waiting to share. I do not mention my hospitalization or explain why I brought a walker with me because I do not want him to worry. When I am finished, I look at my phone. I have been with him for over forty-five minutes. I do not know how to leave. We would never say goodbye. He always said, *See you soon*, and I always responded, *Be safe, love you.*

When I open my fists, I find soggy tissues crumpled in my palms—tissues I do not remember reaching for or using. They just appear in my hands, these sodden, white masses.

I stand up but I cannot say anything. My throat is closed over. Instead, I shimmy. It is something I do when I feel alien in my body, or hungry, or just plain playful. I only dance like this at home, with him, and only really because Kurtis loves it. He dances crooked and silly and with total abandon. He dances while cooking, or in the middle of arguments, or just because. Often, I am drawn into the movement too, compelled by his pure pleasure.

This is how I leave him: dancing backward—so I can see him until the doors close—hands tight on my walker so I will not fall.

61

At Flamenco Fest, our conversation is good but the music does not improve. Yet as we walk back to the car, he insists the music wasn't so bad. We are blocks from the festival then. All its sounds have faded away. We are in the middle of a gravel parking lot. This is when Kurtis leans over and looks at me, holds out his hand, asks me to dance.

There's no music, I say.

No, he disagrees with me, *I can still hear it.*

I take his hand, let him spin me around. I cannot hear what he can but this does not matter because he is with me.

I can't imagine what you are going through, they say. *I just can't.*

Really? I think. You can't?
You have never been in pain?
You have never lost something you loved and never gotten it back?
You really have nothing to work with here?
You can't even try?

Of course, I just nod.

Yes, I say, *it is very hard.*

63

The day of his cremation, I walk right to the casket, touch him, beg him to rise, scare the living day-lights out of me. He would try to startle me in the apartment—jumping out from behind doors, arms waving—but I never spooked.

I'll get you one day, he would say.

This is the third time I have seen his body since he died. After the casket is sealed but before I descend in the elevator to the crematorium, a woman warns me it is an industrial space. This is an understate-ment. The elevator doors open onto a windowless concrete room dominated by a huge cremation chamber.

The chamber's corrugated metal door is rolled up. I can see the slate shadow of the interior. The casket is lifted on a hydraulic platform and slowly trans-ferred into darkness. The metal door rolls down and locks. The woman asks if I want to push *the button*. The button is affixed to the side of the cham-ber, green and egregiously large. White letters on it read START. I walk toward the button. This is the furthest I can go with him. When the cremation begins, it fills the entire room, my ears, my head, my everything with the sound of its roaring.

It's difficult to hear, they say.

It's too heavy.

I can't take it in all at once. It makes me too sad. I need a break.

I am just telling them what happened. I am just telling them how I am doing. I am just telling them he died.

I have to protect my light, someone I have known a long time says. *I can't hear about this all the time if it's always going to be this sad.*

He finds me crying in my bedroom closet. I am sitting below the hems of my dresses, my knees drawn to my chest. I am naked. We have been dating a few months. We are supposed to go out with his friends; I cannot find anything to wear.

Nothing looks right on me, I say.

He tells me it doesn't matter what I wear, I always look beautiful. He reaches out his hand, tells me to let him help me up. He swipes my tears off my puffy face.

Tell no one about this, I command because it is so hard for me to say *I need you*. Even when it is right there, throbbing beneath my chest: I need you, I need you, I need you.

It will be good for you to return to teaching soon, they say. *It will help.*

I consider the complexities of education: planning, assessing, reporting, interacting, and on. I consider myself: reminded to shower, to brush my teeth, to eat, to speak.

The routine of work will be a helpful distraction, they add.

They think I am wallowing but stop short of using the word.

I do not respond. I am in pain so intense it is laughable, entirely improbable, that anything could help.

Every morning for months: a blood thinner and a Valium, dry-swallowed. With my walker, hobbling to the bathroom of my parents' guest bedroom. Staring at myself in the mirror, speaking: *You are here because your husband is dead. He is not coming back.*

The morning of his memorial, I add: *You will say what you have to say.*

Kurtis loved when I told people about him. He would ask me what I said and how. He would beam the whole time I recounted my exact words. This is why I speak at the memorial.

He would have wanted you to do what was best for you, RJ says.

RJ is worried about me speaking. For one, without my walker, I can barely stand upright for three minutes, my leg weak from the AngioJets. For two, RJ thinks it will be too difficult emotionally.

I can't cry, I say. *If I cry, I won't be able to speak.*

Growing up, if I thought I was going to cry in public, I squeezed my hands into fists and pictured

myself standing in an empty grey room sur-
rounded by metal doors. I would imagine locking
the doors. If this did not work, I pinched the skin of
my inner thighs as hard as I could.

Kurtis cries with me more than anyone else. He
opens me up.

I like to think I'm the heart, he says.

Of course you are, I say. *You keep us tender.*

My father's mother is a widow for most of her life, though I never give this fact any real thought until I become one too. She never remarries.

She visits Kurtis and me a year after we move in together. Her hair is perfectly coiffed, a pleasing swirl of black and white grey. We show her the newly painted walls of the apartment, our furniture.

She is dead by the time I become a widow too. Later, I learn her mother was a widow for most of her life as well. I imagine us in a line, a legacy of widows.

Do you worry a piano will fall on your next partner's head?

A woman asks me this after I tell her about the widowhood in my lineage. We are strangers, the woman and I. A mutual friend introduces us at an art opening. There is death in her family, that is why I told her about mine. I wonder if she is joking or not. I wonder if she knows if she is joking or not.

He always wants to know what I think. He is always asking me questions:

How was your day?
What did you teach?
What did you write about?
How tired are you?
Want me to cook?
Should we order za tonight?
Do you want more of the blanket?

There are bigger questions too:

What do you think about my career?
How should I love myself?
Do you think we will still have this much fun together when we are old?

At the memorial, I sit straighter than I ever have before. My entire body is tight. No part of my back or spine touches the chair. I am dry-eyed the whole time. I do not allow myself to cry. I say what I want to say.

For a week after, I writhe with migraine. Grief finds its way through all my defenses. All the sorrow I held at bay in order to speak at the service burns through my brain, red-hot.

70

One sun-filled morning in a November long past, I emerge from the shower. My wet hair is tied up and a grey towel is wrapped around my body. I walk out of our apartment's bathroom and look right, instinctively, toward the front window.

A man has his face pressed against the glass. He is in shadow and I cannot see the details of his face, just the outline of his head, his shoulders, his torso. I yelp, calling for Kurtis. There is no answer. The man at the window beckons for me to come closer. I squint, trying to see more clearly. Water streams down my legs, pooling on the carpet. I recognize the dark sunglasses, the wool jacket, the striped scarf.

Kurtis? I ask.

Somewhere, through speakers he rigged up while I was showering, music starts to play.

I never thought marriage would happen for me, so I have no preconceived notions about a proposal. Still, I never thought I would cry.

The second the music begins, I start to sob. Big, hoarse, wild.

Outside, Kurtis holds up a massive sheet of card stock. In thick black Sharpie he has written a love letter. I read it through the window between us and then he changes the card, reveals another behind it, and then another.

At some point, the towel drops away from my body. My hair falls out of its makeshift knot. He does not so much as pause. When he gets through all the cards, he gestures to the front door. I open it and light rushes inside. He kneels in the snow outside and asks me to marry him.

It is a rare—perhaps even the only—moment in my life where I feel joy and excitement so clear, so immediate, so intense I am not aware of anything else happening to me or around me.

When the memorial service ends, I limp toward the exit. My hands shake. Outside, someone sits on the concrete ledge of a raised planter bed running the length of the building. I recognize Brayden's grey blazer, the mass of his dark red curls. He hugs me and I cry darkness into the shoulder of his jacket.

You did good, he says. *You did good.*

All the things people give us that we do not know we need until we have them.

Do you have independent life insurance contracts?

I ask all my friends, close and far and best and not best. When they say *no*, I tell them though we meant to, we decided to wait until we moved to Vancouver. We thought we had time. I tell my friends how much it costs to die.

When my friends do not take out their phones to make notes, I tell them when your life falls apart, it helps to have money. That is ugly but all of it is.

Do you have a will? I ask them.

Kurtis and I delayed getting one of those as well. When my friends shake their heads, I tell them a lawyer is expensive and a registry more afford-able—either will do. They nod, but I know they do not really hear me.

The policy and the will are not about the dead, I explain.

I am trying to warn them but they are checking the time. They are making sure they will not be late because out there in the elsewhere, someone awaits their return. None of my friends are thinking about the things I am thinking about.

Just over a year after he dies, I am in an airport. I do not get any snacks or water because I do not want to lose my seat outside my gate. The airport is busy, seats are limited. Because of the pandemic, I have been in very few public places since Kurtis's death. Certainly, I have been nowhere this packed with people, none of whom are him.

I am flying to Los Angeles to visit Selene. I have not seen her in person since Kurtis was alive. She invited me to stay with her the month before, wondered if I wanted to leave the city for the one year anniversary. I booked my ticket while I was talking with her on the phone.

In the airport, I do not speak to anyone because I am not with anyone. I am crying but so are others. One woman weeps without blinking, her green eyes huge and fixed.

I take stock of what I am wearing: black N95, black joggers, black sweatshirt, white sneakers. These are the sneakers I wore the day he—

No, I say out loud.

I shake my head. I do not want to fall into re-membering. Crying is painful enough. I look around. I catalogue the snacks people are eating: chocolate coins, cheese puffs, bacon bits, lettuce, popcorn.

That's his favorite—

No.

No, no, no.

One morning in my parents' living room, while they are at work, I kneel on the hardwood floor below his urn, which sits on the small table beside the couch. I beg him to come back. I am almost screaming.

My eyelids gum together, my throat thickens. I cry on the floor for hours, but I only realize this when I look at my phone. Salt dries in a thick, white crust beneath my chin. I scrub that pale rind with a tissue until my skin burns.

RJ tells me a window into this early, acute pain has to be opened, even just a little each week. If this window stays closed, eventually it will seal and the body will adjust to the pain, grow used to its weight.

You are so young, RJ tells me. *Do not carry this your whole life.*

My whole life? I think. What about his whole life?

My first grief-specific counsellor is a woman
named Michelle. She is part of a provincially
funded grief therapy program for people whose
immediate family members have died.

It is the only public-access program of its kind in
the entirety of Canada.

I begin the program online about two and a half
months after he dies. COVID prevents us from meet-
ing in person. Over video chat, Michelle speaks
slowly, with little intonation. Her hair is not cut
into a shape I can identify. She tells me the first six
months of grief put the body into fight-or-flight.
Cortisol floods the system and the brain moves
into a basic protective stance. During this time, the
frontal lobes quiet down—these being the parts of
the brain responsible for cognitive skills such as
emotional expression, problem-solving, memory,
attention, planning and judgment, as well as com-
munication. Blood is drawn away from these
parts of the brain and sent to the parts of the brain
that command basic survival. She reads the

information off digital slides that she screen-shares with me.

I nod along. I have noticed grief severely restricts my attention, a condition I call "grief brain." Michelle asks if I am experiencing any anger.

No, I say. *Just so much sadness.*

She tells me as fight-or-flight begins to ease around six months, I will start to feel a fuller range of emotions.

Usually in months six through nine, she says, *emotions heighten and diversify. This can make these months feel worse than others.*

Worse? I say. *No, I can't take worse.*

One of Kurtis's friends from university tells me we talked on the phone for over an hour the week after Kurtis died.

We did? I wonder because I do not remember.

It's okay, he says. *When my wife asked how you were after I hung up, I told her your voice sounded strange. It sounded like you were floating, like you weren't really there.*

While hospitalized to treat the deep vein thrombosis and pulmonary embolism, I am also diagnosed with something else. I have May-Thurner syndrome: my left iliac vein is compressed by the right iliac artery. The vascular surgeon tells me this compression in my body is responsible for a clot much older than the clots currently in my leg and lungs. In fact, the clot caused by my May-Thurner syndrome has been in my body so long that a web of compensatory veins has grown around it.

The vascular surgeon informs me the first priority is to clear the newer clots in my leg, but in the future, I may require the insertion of a venous stent at the compression site, where the older clot is located. He wants to *keep an eye on me*. He tells me if I ever get pregnant, my May-Thurner syndrome will classify me as high-risk. At this, I laugh and at the sound of my barking, the surgeon does not.

Christopher, one of Kurtis's oldest friends, shows me a plastic skeleton he has purchased to use as a Halloween decoration.

We are sitting on the front stoop of Christopher's house. The skeleton sits too, on its own stair.

Until Kurtis died, Christopher and I never really spent any time together. I suggest naming the skeleton Kurtis, which causes Christopher to cry.

Too dark, he says. *Too soon.*

I apologize. It has been two months since Kurtis died. Death has warped my ability to be in the world. I do not understand how this ornament of death can sit so easily between us but I cannot mention real death—Kurtis's death.

I have become someone I do not understand, that others do not understand. I do not know the right way to be anymore.

Grief counsellor Michelle emails me an information packet about grief. As I start to read it, I learn there is a difference between the realities of grief and what is generally understood about it.

The packet outlines that people tend to believe grief follows a natural cycle characterized by predictable stages, with the acceptance of loss marking the end of the cycle. Apparently, it is also held that "normal" acute grief lasts four to six months before beginning to lessen.

Grief—like mine, like many people's—stretching beyond this time frame is termed "complicated" or "prolonged." The materials in the packet emphasize that though these terms suggest otherwise, there is nothing abnormal about acute grief lasting upward of years.

Because of the AngioJets and because of May-Thurner and because of grief, I am awash in medical appointments. I cannot keep track. I arrive at my family doctor's office at 11:30 only to be told the appointment is at 1:30. My mother drives me because I still physically cannot, and also I am worried I will not remember anything the doctor says to me.

I have several prescriptions I have not needed before: for sleep, for panic, for pain. The sleeping pill gives me copper mouth—after swallowing it, everything I drink tastes like pennies. At other appointments, for other things, doctors ask me what medications I am currently taking but I cannot remember any of the pills' names. My mother fishes a hard-copy list of my medications out of her purse while I stare at the doctors wordlessly. When I do speak, the voice that comes from me is unlike any I have heard emerge from my mouth: slow, heavy, dull.

You need something to hope for, RJ tells me.

What might that be? I say. *Death?*

He shrugs. I laugh, but not really. I tell him I have been looking for a place to die. I have found a mountain called Nameless and a lake called Disappointment.

Where? he wants to know.

Google Maps, I say.

I tell him the pain of loss obliterates everything. I tell him I might drown in Disappointment. He does not laugh.

How can he be gone? I ask.

I don't know, my therapist responds, tears in his eyes.

I bite my tongue until it bleeds, stuff a tissue directly into my mouth.

In another session with grief counsellor Michelle, she tells me there is typically a heightening of acute grief around one year, and sometimes around years three through five.

YEAR five? I gasp.

I grip the piping on my parents' green couch so tightly I bend part of my fingernail. It has been five excruciating months since he died.

Grief is a long journey, Michelle says flatly.

She is a head on shoulders in a rectangle on my laptop screen.

I hear Michelle say something about grief being work, about needing to honor the body's need for rest, but I am not entirely focused.

I can't do this for five years, I think.

Also, I hate Michelle's haircut.

I count, to the day, when I will be the age Kurtis was when he died. I think maybe that is a good time for the bridge that is high enough. When I do the math, the day I land on is my father's birthday.

So, I think, maybe not.

When the day comes, the day I am as old as he was, I realize I have made an error. My father's birthday was the day before.

Week after week, I sit to write a letter about my grief, just as I told RJ I would. I prop my AngioJet'ed leg up on a pillow, open the clamshell of my computer. I never think there are words for what I am feeling but somehow, each time, I begin to type.

I need to convert his checking account to an estate account. I have all these documents: death certificate, Letter of Administration, his banking information, my driver's license. The Letter of Administration is required when someone dies without a will. I have to call and make an appointment to go into the bank. On the phone, the man verifies all the information I provide and then says, *I just noticed his age. So young.* He asks what happened.

I take a deep breath.

I don't know, I say. *His heart stopped.*

Not COVID? the man asks.

No, I say. *Not COVID.*

At the appointment, inside the bank, the woman helping me says, *I'm sorry for your loss.*

I nod. She asks if she can know how he died.

I don't know, I say. *His heart stopped.*

She asks if it was COVID.

No, I say. *Not COVID.*

She asks for the Letter of Administration. I slide

it through the cutout in the clear plastic divider between us.

Good, she says. *This is what we need.*

Panic swamps my body. I can barely breathe behind my mask. I keep wondering why I am here. This is not my bank.

Some mornings, I forget. I wake up swamped with unease, with the sense that something dark is vanishing around the corner. For a second, I cannot catch the trailing tendrils, cannot pull the shadow into shape.

82

In December, I return to the hospital for an MRI, which will show whether I need a stent placed in my left iliac vein. This is the vein compressed by my right iliac artery. The technician reviews this information with me before settling me onto the white MRI bed. Once I am lying down, the technician asks if I have had an MRI before.

I shake my head.

First time, I say.

The technician slides a white cage over top of me.

This is the scanner, the technician explains.

I am not prepared for the weight of the machine on my body. The technician places earplugs in my ears and headphones over top. The MRI bed moves me into a pale, close tunnel. A rhythmic thumping begins. I feel faintly claustrophobic and a little afraid.

Please hold still, the technician says to me through the headphones.

I stare at a sticker of a green alien in a purple track-suit that is pressed onto the surface of the tunnel just above me. I know the sticker is meant as a comfort. In this liminal space, it is supposed to act as a visual anchor for a person who has little to no control over what is happening. I feel more tired than I ever have.

You are here, I think, training my eyes on the alien's stubby, three fingered hands. You are still here.

83

My phone company keeps calling. They call me at all hours of the day almost every day of the week. After over a month, I finally answer: a customer service representative asks me how I am.

Is this a good time?

My husband is dead, I say. *So, no, it is not a good time.*

The representative offers his condolences. I ask what my phone company wants to talk to me about so persistently.

They want you to upgrade, the representative says.

The representative also tells me I am overpaying on my monthly bill. I paid off my current phone almost a year ago, but as I had not called and adjusted my plan, I was still getting charged phone payments. I tell the representative I'll fix it but it is a year before I do.

After the Angios, the first time I leave the house is for Brayden's birthday. My leg is finally healed enough that I am able to drive myself to the address he provides. Once I arrive, I park and then I walk slowly along the sidewalk until I see Brayden's car. I hear the faint sounds of voices coming from the backyard that is hidden behind the house's white stucco exterior. These voices are attached to bodies, sitting in lawn chairs that are rooted in the earth Brayden and his girlfriend scattered with grass seed in the summer. I imagine the couples in attendance, sitting around the firepit in pairs. Perhaps they brought their children with them.

I lean against the hood of Brayden's car and call him.

I can't do this, I say. *I'm sorry.*

He comes out from behind the house. His flannel shirt is the colors of fall. I do not know how to explain my chronic discord, the push-me-pull-me of my sadness. I want to be invited. I cannot attend. The house is two blocks from the place Kurtis lived when I first met him. The street feels spectral.

85

The MRI reveals I require a stent. The vascular surgeon telling me this says I can take some time to decide if getting the stent is what I wish to do.

I stare at him silently. In my lap, I clench my hands into fists. Internally, I am screaming. I feel besieged by mortality—his, mine, the world's. On the radio that morning, a news reporter says the federal government is calling the necessary lockdown prompted by the COVID-19 pandemic "infinite." The reporter's voice betrays her weariness.

I really need a stent?

Yes, the surgeon replies.

People keep telling me to take it *a day at a time.* At night, I cry until my eyes swell shut. I order things online that arrive in brown cardboard boxes. I unpack books about grieving that I throw across the room as soon as I learn the authors remarried within the first year; a vibrating facial massager I never use because I do not have the energy to figure out how to charge it; merino wool socks; a scalp stimulating hairbrush. I do not remember purchasing any of it, but I must have because it is my name on the shipping label; it is my credit card charged.

Brayden tells me the day Kurtis died, I texted him twice. I only recall texting Brayden once, when I asked him to come drive me home.

He tells me my second text said maybe he shouldn't come. Maybe I would return to the city with my parents. He tells me when he received the second message, he had already been driving toward me for an hour.

Did I ever send a third text telling you I did need you to come?

No, he says. *But I knew.*

I shake my head.

I can't remember any of it, I say.

You were in no state to remember anything, Brayden says.

For months, he adds.

I find it alarming that my recollection of what has happened is incomplete. I cannot see its whole face, its whole breadth. Some parts are just gone.

How much of him have I lost to shock? I wonder. Why do I have to keep losing him over and over?

The idea that acute grief lessens after four to six months—where does it come from?

I cannot find anything explaining the origin. No research, no studies. When I ask grief counsellor Michelle, she shrugs. She does not know a specific reference point either.

Nothing supports that time frame in grief experience or therapy, Michelle says.

This does not answer my question. She is repeating things I have already read in the packet.

For most of our sessions, all grief counsellor Michelle seems to do is review the information she has sent me. For most of our sessions, I stare at her without speaking.

I ask the vascular surgeon how much time I can take to decide if I want the stent. He tells me a few weeks is reasonable. He also warns the vein may be too stenosed—compressed, he explains when I ask—for proper stent placement.

There is no way to know until you're actually in the vein, the surgeon says, shrugging lightly.

I ask if he is really telling me I might endure the entire, invasive procedure only to be told after that it did not work, the vein is too occluded for a stent.

That is definitely a possibility, the surgeon says.

Despite multiple tests, no clear reason for my massive clotting event has been found. This fact, in combination with my May-Thurner syndrome, means that—despite the risk of failure—the surgeon believes trying to place a stent in my vein is the best course of action.

A final pick-up notice comes in the mail from the postal service. It is for Kurtis. I go to the post office and wait in line. When it is my turn, I show the notice to the man at the till. I tell him I am picking up. I have my driver's license ready. He looks at the postal slip and then at my photo ID. I have my answer ready too. I already know what he is about to say.

Nothing matches, he says. *Not the right name.*

I shake my head.

I'm the next of kin, I say. *I'm his wife. His widow.*

Now he shakes his head. I am not sure he is actually listening to the things I am saying.

It has to match, he says.

I can tell I am going to have to say it. It is nine in the morning. I do not want to start the day like this.

He's dead, I say.

What?

The postal worker thinks he has not heard me. He thinks my mask has muffled my voice.

He's dead, I say. *I'm his next of kin.*

He taps his ears.

HE'S DEAD, I say.

I pull up the Death Certificate, the Letter of Administration on my phone.

Proof, I say.

He looks at my phone and then back at me. He disappears into the depths of the office and returns, a white envelope in his hand. He passes the mail to me. I thank him.

Have a nice day, he says.

I close my eyes for a second.

You too, I respond.

At the end of one of our sessions, grief counsellor Michelle says to me: *You must think what has happened to you is very unfair.*

By now, I know Michelle and I are not well matched. She is not answering my questions. She keeps assuming she understands me but she does not. She keeps telling me how I feel instead of asking how I feel. I start to withdraw—answering bluntly, my voice flat.

I don't think about fair or unfair, I tell her, again. *How is that going to help me? It doesn't change the fact that he is still dead.*

92

If you could forget your time with him, would you?

I look at Rebecca, waiting for her response. We are sitting outside on a bench overlooking a valley, the bright ribbon of a river.

No, she says. *Even for all the pain of it, I wouldn't give it up.*

I do not tell her that sometimes, my answer is yes. Sometimes, I do not want to remember anymore. I do not know if it is possible to live without remembering but also, I do not know if I can live with it.

It does not matter, ultimately, because I cannot ever seem to stop the remembering. I can only keep it at a distance for a while. It is a shadow I cannot get beyond.

We marry on a beach named Sugar. Sun turns lustrous on the surface of the ocean. The afternoon before the wedding, he and I ride a wave all the way to the shore together, him on his surfboard, me on mine. He reaches the sand first.

The next day, we stand beneath an arch draped with white roses. He stands so straight, his shoulders a perfect line beneath his dark blue suit. We hold each other's hands gently but firmly.

Let time be tender toward us, I say to him. *Let the dishes sit in the sink, let the radio play your favorite song, let the moon pull the tides at will, and, oh, let love be at the end, wherever that may be.*

I worry we might divorce. Not that he will die.

I learn in grief therapy that, statistically, most widows and widowers lose over half their support base in the first year of loss due to grief-attrition. Which is to say, the relentless intensity of grief wears people out.

Around month six, I recall grief counsellor Michelle warning me that acute grief can intensify now or in the next few months. I start to worry my pain will terminally exhaust the people supporting me.

In my daily life, I begin to emphasize what I imagine people will interpret as Good Signs: smiling, showering, joke-making, eating vegetables, asking how people's children are doing. I want to be easier to be around, so people will stay around.

You're in good spirits, one friend says when he sees me.

I do not tell him or anyone about all the nights I sob into a towel in the bathroom.

It's so tiring, Rebecca says, *doing so much alone.*

It has been just over a year since Rebecca's husband died. We are walking her sleek black dog along the edge of the park near Rebecca's apartment. I tell Rebecca I am sick of hearing: *You're so strong. I don't know how you handle this loss so well.*

We talk about the Good Signs that other people tend to conflate with inner strength: getting a job, moving out on your own, going on solo hikes, planning a vacation, putting on makeup, brushing your hair, going on a date.

Rebecca and I have each done some of these things. Yet neither of us goes a day without thinking life is not worth living. Neither of us knows how to continue without the people that chose us.

After dating for three weeks, I tell Kurtis he better stop seeing other people. He turns from the stove where he is watching macaroni noodles and powdered cheese combine in a steel pot. He claps his right hand to his chest.

I'm not dating anyone else, he says. *Why would you think that?*

I stare at him. He is so sincere but then again so am I. No one has ever just wanted me before. He is the first person I do not have to convince. I mention none of this to him. I am embarrassed by my own need. I try to hide its soft yearning with hard demands.

I don't want to waste my time, I tell him. *I want something that lasts.*

I ask if he can commit to that.

When I tell my friends what I have said, they say I am crazy.

Play it cool, they say. *You've only been dating a month.*

I remind them I am not cool, even though it is obvious.

You are too much, they say, laughing.

That is what I am afraid of, but I do not tell them that.

I read more about grief. It takes me hours to understand three or four sentences. This is because I cannot sustain attention. I read the word "death" and I forget it immediately. I have to go back and read the word, the sentence, the paragraph again. I read and reread, trying to understand.

I learn the Five Stages of Grief—denial, anger, bargaining, depression, acceptance—were never meant to describe the experiences of the bereaved. The stages arose out of a non-evidence-based study that considered the emotional experiences of people diagnosed with terminal illnesses.

When I read this, I think I have misunderstood. I have seen the Five Stages of Grief my entire life. I read the passage again; my grief brain is not interfering with my comprehension. The Five Stages were never meant to apply to those grieving the death of a loved one. They were meant for another kind of pain.

Writing about my grief is so agonizing, so exhausting I always think I will need to stop. Yet, I do not.

It is the only thing I feel able to do since he died. The only way I am able to say what it is like for me. The only place I can meet grief without being utterly consumed by it.

When I first return to the apartment Kurtis and I lived in, it has been six months since his death. I enter the apartment with my friends Brayden and Katie. We have all known one another for years. Katie arrives last but when she sees me and Brayden, she gives us each a long hug. She is the kind of person who holds on tight.

I ask my friends to help me gather Kurtis's things and move them into storage at my parents' place because I am worried about further wearying my family. I still live with my parents and my sister still comes over after work to check on me.

As I enter the apartment and then walk through the hallway toward Kurtis's study, I want to throw up.

The barf test: that is what my new grief counsellor Ann calls it.

If it makes you want to vomit, she says, *don't do it.*

Grief counsellor Michelle has taken a stress leave. This is how I end up with Ann. I hope Michelle will be all right but I do not want her to return to work. I like Ann so much better than Michelle.

In therapy, Kurtis and I each write a list of things that bother us about the other. The lists are private, shared only with RJ in separate sessions. At home I poke Kurtis's shoulder lightly.

Tell me, I say. *Tell me, tell me, tell me.*

When he won't, I guess.

I'm petty, I say. *I'm a homebody. I'm intense. I'm melancholic.*

What's melancholic? he asks.

I don't hang out with your friends much, I say. *I've never tried coffee and that's psychopathic.*

At this, he laughs, but no matter how many times I ask, he will not tell me what is on his list.

Drop it, RJ tells me but I cannot.

101

I am packing up Kurtis's things because I want to live in the apartment again but I cannot do that with his possessions still in place, as if he has gone away on a trip and will be back soon.

Kurtis's study is beside our bedroom, but I do not look in there. Instead, I train my eyes on the door of the study as it swings open. Katie walks in first, then me, Brayden following behind.

The study is a mess. His mess. I swallow the sting of stomach acid. My mother and my sister are the only people who have been in the apartment since he died. Months ago, they collected some of my clothes for me, enough that I could live at my parents' place, which is ten minutes away. Otherwise, the apartment has been left alone—all our things, his things, untouched. I know the stasis of the apartment is possible because my landlord generously insisted on pausing my rent payments for a year.

At night, he makes the bed with me in it. He grumbles about the sheets he claims I mess up.

The way you sleep, he says. *It's a full twist and shout.*

I insist he is not right but the sheets are still a tornado when he is not there.

On Valentine's Day, I get dinner with a friend. It has been three days since what should have been Kurtis's thirty-third birthday. I am raw with grief, running ragged on two hours of sleep. Still, before dinner, I blow-dry my hair, pat eye shadow onto my eyelids.

Good Signs, I think as I thread silver hoops through my earlobes.

You look lovely, my friend says when she sees me.

We talk for a while, order wine. When my friend asks if I have started thinking about dating, I try to deflect with a weak joke about no one wanting to date a widow. I expect my friend to shake her head or laugh politely but this is not what she does.

Hey, my friend says to the server, *Amy here is a widow and whenever she feels like getting back out there—*

Not anytime soon, I say.

BUT, my friend continues, *if she does, would you consider it a problem that she's a widow?*

The server's eyes are shocked above his mask. I feel a little sorry for him. People do not know what to do with the word *widow*. They do not know where to put their hands.

Well, the server says, *it depends.*

On what? my friend asks.

It is evident to me the conversation is not going the way my friend thought it would.

I guess on whether you killed your husband or not, the server says.

Neither my friend nor I laugh.

No, I say, *I didn't kill him. He just died very suddenly.*

I can almost see the crater the server wishes would open beneath his feet.

That's awful, he says. *I wouldn't consider it a problem. No.*

My friend grins, embattled but triumphant.

After the server leaves, I go to the bathroom. When I return, my friend tells me the server came over in my absence and apologized.

He thinks he offended you, she says. *He told me he actually thinks you seem really nice.*

I think about the server apologizing to my friend. How afraid he is of me. I have so many Good Signs and he is still so afraid.

Loneliness has always dogged me. I cannot ever recall not feeling this way. It ashamed me, how dependent it made me on him. I would try to deny it.

I need my space, I would tell him. *You can't be around all the time.*

He would listen to me. He would stop texting, stop asking questions, stop coming over and cooking me dinner. I would call him, freaking out.

Are we breaking up? I would ask. *You said you wouldn't.*

The first time a short story I have written is published, Kurtis has been dead for almost seven months.

I read an early version of the story to him the year before. I sit on the kitchen counter while he uses two forks to shred roast chicken. When I am finished, he says: *It's so good, baber. When it gets published, we're going to drink a bottle of the very best bubbles.*

I will not let myself imagine selling the story, but it is enough for me that he can.

Maybe you need to find somewhere new to live, RJ says.

I insist that cannot be the case. The apartment was my home with him for so long. I need it to be my home again.

When Katie opens the closet doors in Kurtis's study, I see what remains: his brown cowboy hat, the one he wore on our third date; his red hiking backpack my family bought him at the holidays; his red and black helmet he wore as he biked to and from work every day; his bag of art supplies, bought when we took a painting class together. I pull the hat and the helmet out of the closet, hold them close to my body. Katie asks how she and Brayden can help me.

Let's start with his bookshelves, I say.

Inwardly, loss turns its blade in my flesh but I do not cry. I do not want to make things worse for my friends who move around softly, speaking in quiet voices, the way they would in church or at a funeral. I do not want to wear them out.

Later, on a walk with Katie around the reservoir, she tells me she has to remind herself I am grieving.

You have such a good poker face, Katie says. *Sometimes I forget you are in pain and then I remember.*

I smile.

Crippling pain, I say.

Kurtis and I fill in a personality questionnaire together.

Do you think your partner is secretive? he reads out loud.

He looks at me.

Don't be mad, he says, as he circles YES.

105

I decide to have the stent placed into my body.

I know this choice will be taken as a Good Sign. I want to offer this to the people who have so steadfastly loved me since Kurtis died. I also have another reason for agreeing to the stent but this reason I tell no one.

When I phone the vascular surgeon to inform him of my decision, the surgeon tells me the hospital's scheduling team will call me in a few weeks to let me know when I am booked in for the procedure.

Can't wait, I say.

The experience of grieving makes it clear to me that grief does not occur in predictable stages with obvious endpoints. It is, however, a relief to learn the famous Five Stages were not meant to describe my grief. This means I am not doing something wrong.

I find the more I learn of the commonly held beliefs about grief, the more I cannot understand how such grossly reductive and inaccurate ideas about bereavement can exist.

How can grief be so universal and yet still so widely misunderstood?

107

Kurtis sits for hours in his study playing music, headphones on, instruments plugged in, sheet music displayed on his tablet.

In another life, he tells me one time. *I become a musician first.*

I know he is playing when I come home after teaching and his shoes are in the entryway but the apartment is silent. I pad down the hallway and lean against the door frame, watch him press the keys of his electric piano, or strum the strings of his guitar, his hands moving nimbly. When he turns and sees me watching, he pulls his headphones off. He asks me if I will listen to what he has been working on. I listen to him play and feel knots unfurl in my body that I do not know I am tied up in.

After hours organizing Kurtis's things, eventually Katie and Brayden fill their vehicles with his instruments, boxes of his clothes. As they shuttle Kurtis's possessions to my parents' house, I stay in the office and pull a plastic bin out from the back of the closet.

Inside the bin, Kurtis has kept all the cards I gave him, dating back to the month we met. There are photobooth strips from New Year's Eves, staff parties, music festivals, malls, bars. There are 4x6 photographs of us through the years and every professional photo and Polaroid from our wedding, stacked neatly. There are pamphlets from art shows we attended, museums we visited. There are two tickets to a film screening, tickets we never used, always intending to go and then never quite making it. There are the little notes I used to write to him on scrap paper, just because. There is my thesis from my master's degree, which he bound into a book, the cover his own design.

I sort through all of it. He is everything, he is nothing. Pain seethes in my body, but I still have not let myself cry in the apartment in front of Katie and Brayden. My head hurts terribly.

One night, in his sleep, Kurtis sneezes directly into my face.

Some evenings, I fall asleep listening to Kurtis play acoustic guitar on the side of our bed. Other times, after I buy him a banjo, he gives me a one-man-show; he plays the banjo, the harmonica, the tambourine. He sings about slow dancing, about growing old, about the wind and the rain. Most nights, though, he stays up late creating electronic tracks on his tablet, tracks he plays for me later, while we make dinner.

Beats and Eats, he calls it.

It's so quiet, I say to Katie when she asks how I am feeling.

Katie and I are on one of our Sunday walks. She goes with me every week for more than a year, regardless of the weather. Her husband takes care of their child while she and I are together—a kindness that is not lost on me.

I can't get past it, I say. *It's just completely silent.*

110

When I receive a copy of the literary journal that published my short story, I hold it in my hands and cry.

Kurtis would have leapt around the apartment yelling. He would have bought a copy for every single person he knew. He would have stood, beaming, over their shoulders as they read it.

I am not going to do any of those things. It is not just because he is dead. I have never been the kind of person that can jump for joy—I want to but I am always too afraid. I need him to feel it for me. Jump for me.

After moving Kurtis's things out of the apartment, I start to spend days there. This goes poorly. I keep collapsing in panic and fear. Around me our life echoes in the walls, the shower, the carpet, the kettle.

The apartment is the last place I felt like myself; I hope to find myself there again. I convince myself somehow, impossibly, the pain I find in the apartment will change. It is so hard to choose the unknown over the known and I do not want to choose. What I know, though painful, is something I love with tangible intensity.

On a Saturday, Kurtis gives up his grey sleep T-shirt, which he has worn since his early teens. It is so old it is disintegrating, holes sagging under the armpits, the collar separating from the shirt. On that weekend, the last one before he dies, we are in bed. I catch the collar of his T-shirt with my hand. When he looks at me, his eyes big and bright, almost laughing, and says, *Don't you dare*, I do. I pull.

The shirt tears into pieces, which he proceeds to tie around his body. He dances around our bedroom while "I Will Remember You" plays on his phone. I film him dancing with the T-shirt and the frame shakes with my laughter. On our bed is a pile of his laundry, the tops of my toes, the crumple of our quilt.

The first time I use the car wash after his death, I feel like my chest is caving in. Days before he died, he took my car and filled it with gas. Only to be kind. When he brought my car home, he told me he had gifted me a car wash, had curled the long, white receipt bearing the code for a luxury wash in my cupholder.

Make sure to go soon, baber, he said.

When I finally do go, he has been dead for months. As I exit the wash, the shout of the commercial dryer behind me, the sun is in my eyes. It is months before I can bear to clean my car again.

A few weeks before I meet Kurtis, I go on a date with someone who asks me to climb into his bedroom closet when he hears his roommate come home. I sit, my legs crossed, and peer through the closet slats. I think how funny this story will be to tell my friends. I do not feel pity for myself. It never occurs to me I would not be someone who should be hidden away. When I tell Kurtis this story, he looks at me, his eyes huge.

Amy, he says gently.

He reaches out to touch me. I recoil, not from him, but from what he is offering. This tenderness I want but do not know how to receive.

We fight one night. It is a Friday. Mid-argument, I leave the apartment, slam the door behind me. I drive around the city until my breathing slows. He keeps calling me but I will not answer. When I return to the apartment, he is not there. I sit on our couch and listen to one of the voice mails he has left on my phone: *Hey, baber, I'm worried about you. Please call me back.*

I do not call him. When he returns, I ask him where he went.

Everywhere, he says. *Looking for you.*

The night I storm out of our home and he goes searching for me, we have been together for years. I know he loves me, but when he goes after me, he shows me he loves me in a way that answers a question I have been asking my whole life.

When a woman from the hospital calls to tell me the date of my stent insertion, I am in the middle of removing Kurtis from all our jointly networked streaming accounts.

I put the woman on speakerphone. She tells me the procedure will be in two weeks. Someone needs to drive me home from the hospital, nothing to eat or drink twelve hours before, check-in at the front desk upon arrival. The whole time she is speaking, I am navigating the settings section of yet another application.

I have to remove him from so many accounts. The woman says something about where the front desk is found but she is speaking routinely, too quickly. I do not catch the desk's location before the call ends. After she hangs up, I have to continue my task.

Delete user? Confirm.

Delete user? Confirm.

Delete user? Confirm.

The increase in sorrow that grief counsellor Michelle warned me about finds me in month seven. This is also the month in which my stent insertion is scheduled.

I do not want to admit how much pain I am in because I am still trying to emphasize Good Signs in an attempt to not tire out my loved ones. As a result, I do not tell anyone when I collapse in the hallway of my parents' house one day. I try to breathe evenly but fail. No one is home except for me. Alone, I allow myself to really feel an ache so intense I wonder how my skin and bones contain it. I curl up on the carpet as small as I can, begging my body to let me stand back up. I cannot get enough air between my sobs to find a way to say out loud: I am not going to make it.

117

The day before my stent insertion, I receive an email. The subject line reads: Puppy.

The sender is the dog breeder he and I chose the year before. I open the email:

Red sable puppy, female, she's yours if you want her. Ready to go in two months.

I did not expect it. I had forgotten he and I were on the spring list. I wonder if I can take this puppy and care for it without him. I wonder if I want to. I cry. He would have felt joy I cannot and his elation would have drawn out mine, heightened it even. Together we would have planned how to tell everyone we were getting a dog. I cry because grief finds its way into everything, makes everything a part of itself.

I hit REPLY and type:

I'll take her.

Immediately, a new email pings into my inbox. No words, just a picture of a curled-up, dark red puppy.

I want to want the dog but looking at the photo, I only feel hollow.

As the pain of grief continues to worsen, I think increasingly about dying.

What do you think will happen if you die? RJ asks. *Do you believe in heaven?*

Not anymore, I tell him.

You used to? he asks.

I tell RJ my family is religious. I was born into Christianity—into the belief heaven existed. Still, even as a young girl I used to have what I now realize were small anxiety attacks about the idea of eternal life. I could not understand why it comforted my parents that death was not an end. My chest would seize at the thought of never ceasing to exist. I would lie in bed at night and think about continuing forever. I would have such a hard time breathing I would have to count on the inhale, count on the exhale.

Did you think about death a lot when you were young? RJ asks.

Doesn't everyone? I respond.

The first name Kurtis suggests for the new puppy is MoMA, because of our love of art and because he first told me he loved me in New York.

It's perfect, I say and he beams.

120

The day of the stent insertion, my mother drives me to the hospital where I am handed a white-and-blue gown and a pile of warm blankets that I wrap around my shoulders. Beside the hospital bed, my mother settles into a chair and pulls out a pair of socks for me. She always thinks like that—of others, of how to take care of them.

Eventually, my blood is drawn, an IV inserted into my arm. Little black x's for my pedal pulses are drawn with a marker onto my feet, the socks stripped away in favor of blue surgical booties. Then I am back in the cold room where I have been before for my AngioJets. Then I am on the table. Then general anesthetic wipes everything away for the moment.

As a child, I thought the oblivion of death would be a relief. Life without limit seemed like a kind of hell.

After the procedure to insert the stent concludes, I sleep in recovery until I am released from the hospital. The vascular surgeon visits me once more before I leave. He tells me the stent was placed in an almost-ideal location.

Everything looks great, he says.

My mother drives me home amid a thick scattering of white snowflakes. I watch the snow dizzy around the car. I think about how, if he had been here, he would have been so concerned, asking all these questions I would not know how to answer. He would be waiting for me, wherever our home was, his dark eyes still and serious, the way they were when he was really worried. He would have fussed as I settled into bed, where I would be for a while. My leg is tender and fragile. My healing requires that it be held straight and not taxed for some time. He would have insisted on taking time off work to care for me. Always, he took care of me.

121

I log in to one of Kurtis's online shopping accounts to deactivate it. In his cart, I discover a small, wooden beard comb that he has saved. He grew more facial hair than ever before during the first five months of the pandemic. He was inordinately proud. I stare at the hopeful comb he will not order and then I put my head down and cry so much and so long my tears pool on the desk, eventually weeping off the edge.

When I tell my friend Selene this—she is still calling me every day to write with me—I tell her though the crying sounds like an exaggeration, it is not. I really am still crying this hard, for this long.

I shouldn't have accepted the puppy, I tell RJ. *I can't do it without him. It's too much.*

He tells me I can take my yes back, turn it into a no, or a not-yet. I shake my head. I feel compelled to keep the dog. I have already agreed. It is the dog he and I would have received.

This is the first future-think you've done, RJ says.

I inform him I have already squared it with my mother that if I die, she will have to take care of the dog.

Still, RJ says. *It is.*

I shrug. I do not want to live, but for the sake of my family and my friends, I am trying to want to. That is what the dog is to me.

122

Rebecca tells me she hopes for a bus that does not see her, fatal rock fall while on a hike. I do not want any of that. If I die, I tell her, I want to die because I choose to. I want to climb the last height and confront its awesome length. I want to feel the way my body beats against it. I want to tell my body all the pain it has put me through is going to end. That I have brought us to the end.

Does it feel like you have been run over by a train?

This, from the on-call psychiatrist at the urgent psych intake center in the hospital.

No, I say. *You hear a train coming.*

The psychiatrist is very tall; his body is much greater in span than the small office chair he sits upon. He looks directly at me. He does not follow a set list of questions. Instead, he asks me about myself, and after I finish speaking, he responds in kind.

Because of this thoughtful attention, I tell the psychiatrist about the Kurtis-dying, my almost-dying, my wanting-to-die. I tell him about the stent that now resides within my body. I tell him I agreed to the procedure because the vascular surgeon informed me without the stent the chance of another life-threatening clot event is high. I tell him what I have told no one else because I do not want to wear out my loved ones with the truth: the stent is not about trying to live. It is about trying to decide for myself where the end will be.

The grief is so intense, I say. *I feel powerless all the time.*

I talk to the psychiatrist for a long while. Unlike others, he does not try to instruct me on what I should or should not do. What I should or should not feel. Instead, he tells me: *You are clearly the kind of person who will decide for herself.*

The muscles in my shoulders relax when he says this. This is exactly what I want: a sense of agency in a life I feel grief has totally overtaken.

Before I leave his office, the psychiatrist asks if he can give me some advice. When I nod, he hands me a small charm shaped like a turtle.

Go slowly, the psychiatrist says gently.

In my palm, the silver metal warms.

After weeks of keeping my leg as still as possible, I am allowed to start moving around. A small ball of purple scar tissue forms in the skin of my upper thigh. This is where the catheter bearing the stent entered my body. Despite these signs of physical healing, the worsening of my grief continues relentlessly into month eight and then month nine.

I tell my parents, my best friends that I do not intend to live past thirty-five. I tell RJ too. I name the plan Freedom 35. I tell my loved ones about the plan because I want them to know I am serious. I need them to know there is a limit to my capacity for pain. RJ asks if my intentions are absolute. I shake my head on my side of the computer screen. My plan is not fixed. I just do not want to endure this much pain for an indeterminate amount of time.

The pain has to lessen, I tell RJ. *One way or another, I need a path toward less.*

On a Thursday, I try to roll a ball of dough into a pizza base. I cannot get it. The flour lumps, the dough a stringy mess. It is my fault. I used to lean against the kitchen wall and watch him flour the counter, knead the dough, roll it with a pin until it was perfect thin crust. When he offered to teach me, I shook my head.

I don't need to learn, I said. *I have you.*

He always told me: *fifty years, baber, fifty years*. That is how long he felt we would be together. *At least*, he would add. He said it so much at some point I started believing him.

The day I pick up MoMA, it is early May. I have not slept in more than forty hours. She is 2.8 pounds. I am not prepared for her smallness. All the toys I have gotten for her are too big. I hold her in my arms. I tell her my name. I tell her if things had been different, she would have met two people.

He's the better one, I say. *You would have loved him.*

I am shrouded in exhaustion so thick I feel drunk. When I hand the puppy to my mother, she nuzzles MoMA's soft hair. My mother coos. Watching my mother so obviously love MoMA, I cannot feel anything but despair.

I thought Kurtis and I would love the puppy together. Without him, I feel entirely unable. I do not say a word out loud, but I do not feel anything for the puppy at all.

I dream of him only once. In it, his hair is long, the way it was when I first met him. I see him ahead of me, leaning against a doorway. He turns as I approach him. When he sees me, I ask if it is really him.

It really is, he says.

We both know he has come back from the dead. I hold him.

How did you do it? I ask. *How are you here?*

He tells me what he had to do was difficult.

When you go—he looks at me—*just go.*

I ask what he means, what it cost him to come find me. Then, we are in some kind of open-air vehicle. We are sitting beside each other, his shoulder against mine. I am telling him my heavy, my unspeakably painful, the way I used to. The way I need to. He shakes his head as I tell him. It is a small shake, his mouth pressed together softly, the edges of his lips turned up slightly. I have seen it before. I know what it means. It is as much a part of our internal language as anything. He says something after he shakes his head, but the words are lost to me as soon as he speaks them. That does not matter. The head shake tells me everything I need to know. It gives me what I have been looking for.

I tell him it is so good to hear his voice again.

I miss hearing you speak, I say.

He has such a unique cadence to his speech, a light and bouncy way of pronouncing words.

But it's talking to you, sharing things with you that I miss the most, I add.

The vehicle bearing us continues at the same pace but the edges of the dream are thinning. We both know he is going to die again. We sigh deeply over the separation coming for us. Neither of us says anything more. There is not enough time.

We shared a language that was all our own. I am now the last speaker of it.

I do not know what to believe about the dream.

Logically, I say to RJ, *I know the mind is powerful, that I made it up.*

RJ lifts his hands and then lowers them.

Why does it have to be made up? he asks.

I tell him it is not just that I no longer believe in an After. It is that I *cannot* believe in an After if I want to even try to stay alive.

You see, I say, *if it really was him, if there really is an After and he is in it, then I won't stay here.*

I look at RJ encased in his small box on my computer and then I look past the screen to the blank wall of my parents' guest bedroom. I am crying again.

I have to believe there's nothing and that he is nowhere. I have to believe there is no way back to him.

Love makes everything work out.

Kurtis tells me this, over and over. It is his most religious belief.

It doesn't, I say. *Sometimes, love is not enough.*

It is, he says. *You'll see.*

The first time I clip MoMA into her puppy car seat, my arms are full of her things: a bag of puppy kibble, a collapsible water bowl, her chew toys, her blanket, her leash, her harness. I struggle with the snap on the safety belt of the car seat, and my mother, who has walked me out to my vehicle, sees me yelp in frustration: *I CAN'T DO THIS.*

She leaps forward and takes over. I realize I have left my wallet and my keys inside. I am crying but more so because I am exhausted. MoMA wakes up a lot in the night. The ache in my body continues to deepen.

We will see him again.

Christopher says this to me. He has known Kurtis since early childhood. We are downtown, sitting at a restaurant's shiny oak bar. It is late. We are not talking about Kurtis and then we are.

I can't believe that, I tell him.

I have to, he says.

Kurtis didn't believe in heaven, I say. *He didn't believe even a little.*

For the first year Kurtis and I date, I keep asking RJ: *How do you know if you love somebody?*

It is not that I don't know I love him, it is that I want to see around the corner of the universe, to know it will all last.

At the end of May, it is my birthday. Katie and Brayden ask what I would like to do.

Nothing, I think.

Still, we go out for a picnic.

When I show up at the park, MoMA sniffs the air jubilantly. I carry her in my arms and worry it is too hot outside for her small body. Sun is heavy on my arms and legs. Brayden and Katie have brought sparkling wine, vegan cheese, specialty crackers, fancy meats. There are gourmet doughnuts too. I look at the gleaming spread. I know Brayden and Katie love me. I can literally see it in front of me but I cannot feel it. I cannot get to their love—or maybe, it cannot get to me. I keep looking at the sky, which is a cloudless blue bowl, and thinking if I crack open my chest, that is what I will see too. Empty blue.

The year I turn thirty he gets into a minor fender bender because he fills the car so full of balloons he cannot see out of his mirrors.

131

Sometimes, I worry I am wrong and the religion I was raised in is right. Maybe Kurtis is within an After. Maybe consciousness never breaks. Maybe every time I say, *Please come back*, he hears me. It would hurt him, if he could hear me, but I cannot seem to stop asking. I keep putting my plea into the void for which there is no real name.

The dream I have the most is the one where my body traps me. I tell my limbs to move but they will not. I am unable to breathe and no matter how much I try to lift an arm, open my mouth, expand my lungs, I cannot. When I wake, I am thrashing around, gasping for air with a panic that tells me I really was not breathing.

My friend Katie sleeps in the living room on the couch the first time I stay overnight in the apartment. I have not been in our bed since before he died. I watch hours slip by on the clock that has not been set in almost a year. My mouth is dry all night. My nose plugs up. My eyes almost glue shut from crying. Only my arm falls asleep because I leave it outstretched, my fingers pushed through the slats of the dog crate, there for MoMA whenever she needs to smell me with her wet, soft nose.

At 7:30 in the morning, I hear Katie leave through the front door. She needs to return home to check on her daughter and her husband. I am glad she does not see my swollen eyelids, my salt-encrusted cheeks. She has done so much for me. I do not want her to know how much pain I am still in.

Once the apartment falls silent again, I swing my body out of bed and open the crate door. MoMA sniffs at my feet. I realize I have lost the toenail of my left foot's baby toe. The nail was not loose or injured in any way, but now it is separate from my body. I pick up the nail from the carpet and con-sider its small brokenness, its pale curved shell.

May, years ago. It is snowing, which I hate but he insists we go outside.

It's beautiful, he says.

Slow, heavy flakes frost the top of his head.

It's cold, I say.

When I look at him I feel tenderness so close to sadness my eyes burn.

Something is wrong with me, I tell him.

No, baber, he says. *Nothing is wrong.*

The morning after my first time sleeping at the apartment without him, I sit on the edge of the bed, the toenail in my hand. I am sandbagged by tiredness, rocks in my eyes.

Eventually, I hook MoMA into her harness and take her for a morning pee. Outside it is grey, rainy, and cool. In the alleyway behind the apartment the sight of garbage bags, torn open by ravens and magpies—spilling out crumpled receipts, dirty napkins, husks of food packaging—makes my eyes well, my nose stinging. It is not that the ravaged garbage reminds me of him. It is that the bags, the waste, any of it, can still exist and he does not.

Kurtis, I say out loud, but softly, because a man is ahead, pulling his green recycling bin back into his yard.

Please come back, I say.

The man tugging at his bin looks in my direction.

Not you, I think, watching the way the man's garbage bin wobbles over the loose stones of the alleyway. The wheels are rickety, clattering.

That morning, I finally admit to myself that there is no way for me to return to our home. I kept hoping things would be different but the apartment is not ours anymore. There is no way around this fact, no way to stop the pain this fact produces.

The night Christopher and I are out together, our pint glasses leave cloudy rings on the gleaming surface of the bar. I ask him why he believes he will see Kurtis again.

Are you religious? I ask. *Do you think there is an afterlife?*

He tells me he does not believe in any of that. I stare at him. We are both crying.

Then how can you think you will see him again?

He shakes his head.

I will, he says.

No, I say. *He's nowhere. He's gone.*

I will, he says.

Since Kurtis died, Christopher and I have cried together in no fewer than three bars. I wonder if he cries when he is alone. I know Christopher is afraid of fully facing the reality of Kurtis's death. I know he needs something between him and the agony of absence. Because I understand this, I do not say: What we were told about grief before we were in it is wrong.

I do not say: Everyone is so afraid of grief and this fear is dangerous to the grieving. I do not tell him the painful lesson I am learning: Enduring the thing itself—he is not coming back—is unbearable but denying it is worse, is an even greater, even more insidious, threat to living, if that is what you want to do.

During the lockdown prompted by the pandemic, Kurtis and I walk outside each afternoon. Once, we pass a fluffy dog excitedly humping its owner's leg. We draw a wide berth but both of us see the pink flesh of the dog's penis. We both do a double take. Then, we look at each other. I grin because he is already in his glee. The dog turns to look at us because Kurtis is chortling so loudly.

What a filthy, wicked smile he has. What a gleam in his eye.

136

After the first overnight, I stop spending time at the apartment. I never sleep there again. My parents tell me I can live with them for as long as I need. I have been with them for ten months. Ten months since the apartment was his home, was our home.

I let people pray for me. I believe in people's good intentions when they tell me Kurtis is in the afterlife, whatever that may be to that person. I do not want to take away the comfort it brings people to think of him in heaven. I do not tell them for me there can be no such solace.

I do not tell them that, for me, heaven means something entirely different. Means something now impossible, like the pillows that used to be on our bed. Mine: deep grey, his deep blue. He calls my side of the bed *grey zone*. He declares it the better side. Often, I wake to his dark head sharing my pillow.

Hey! I protest. *You have your own side.*

He pats my pillows affectionately and says: *But it's so nice around here.*

One afternoon, I am holding MoMA. It has been ten and a half months since he died. She squirms, wanting to be let down. I bend over, intending to lower her to the ground slowly. Instead, I lose my grip. She falls, striking the concrete sidewalk with the side of her skull. She yelps, so loudly, so sharply, and for so long it feels like she might never stop. I crouch, chest constricting, heart thudding.

No, I say. *Not you, not you.*

I drive her directly to the emergency pet hospital where there is a line. When it is my turn, I take too long explaining to the vet what has happened. My hands are shaking, my voice too. The vet assures me puppies are resilient but I am unconvinced. I insist the vet check her over. While MoMA is assessed inside the clinic, I sit outside in my car and cry, my tears slick on the steering wheel.

I am so afraid MoMA is going to die. I do not realize right away the intensity of this fear means I love her. When I understand, I wonder how I have found a way to love something new. After he died, I did not know if could. I did not know if any fresh love could find a way through the intensity of grief.

139

On Sundays Kurtis and I play board games with my family. There is one involving a cave. The longer a player stays in the cave, the greater the risk of being eliminated by gas leak or snake bite. Yet, the longer a player stays in the cave, the greater the chance of discovering a pile of gold that guarantees a win. Kurtis always lasts longer than us all. He just will not leave the cave. He dies, over and over, inglorious deaths, but he will not stop. Every time the dealer asks if he wants to stay, he says: *Yes, yes. This time it will be my time.*

I do not know what any of us deserve. I know he wanted more.

I go to Mara Lake. I have never been before and I arrive in the dark. The first thing I know of the lake is the way dock lights waver upon the surface in short, cream streaks. As soon as I arrive, Christopher and the guys holler. Christopher's family owns a place in Mara. At his invitation, the guys gather here—an annual late-summer trip. It has been just over a year since Kurtis died. There are twelve guys in total. All of them have known Kurtis since grade school. They group around a picnic table beneath a weeping willow larger than any I have ever seen. Christopher presses a black-handled knife into my hand. I look at the blade in my palm and try not to think about dying. Someone else hands me a beer.

Shotgun, the guys chant.

Christopher mimes using the knife to cut a slit into the side of the silver can.

Shotgun.

Christopher was the best man at Kurtis's and my wedding. The last time Kurtis visited Mara Lake he was attending his bachelor party. He texted me photographs of a lake I now see for myself at night.

When I get somewhere, it is never how I think it will be.

Christopher tells everyone to bring their own groceries to Mara. The town is small, food options are limited. I order my groceries online.

I used to shop for Kurtis and myself. I would walk the aisles searching for his favorite snacks to surprise him. Since his death, I have yet to step foot in a grocery store.

The distance between here and there is the answer to the wrong question.

For most of the first evening at the lake, I sit at the picnic table and watch a pyramid of Junior McChickens dwindle in direct correlation to the number of keg stands performed. During one keg stand, I am asked to work the pump, which I have never done before because I was overly studious at university. I hold the mouthpiece the wrong way and forget, at first, to press the latch down.

I'm not as fun as him, I say.

The guys hesitate but I am not fishing for assurance. It is just true.

No one is as fun as him, they say.

I blink rapidly and stare into the dark. I do not want to cry because that will be embarrassing. They have invited me because they cannot invite him. I do not want them to regret it.

The night Kurtis returns from his bachelor party he is hungover, under-slept, reeking of alcohol. Still, he skips showering so he can sit in bed beside me and type out everything he loved about the weekend. It is an incredibly long note on his tablet. As he writes, he shows me videos of the guys puking into black garbage bags they loop around their ears.

Best bachelor party ever, he says.

He is almost glowing. The list goes in an email that he sends to all the guys.

143

The next morning, we all pile onto a large pontoon boat. Christopher has us leave our shoes in a haphazard pile on the dock. The boat tears through the green glass of the water. When we are in the middle of the lake, Christopher cuts the engine and we drift. At the edge of the nearest shore, which is still many lengths away, steep shale cliffs rise into the sky.

Let's jump, one of the guys says.

I look at the grey slate bluffs and think about Kurtis.

He and I went hiking once. I walked right to the edge of the mountainside while he stayed far away, yelling for me to *come back right now*.

Before the trip, grief counsellor Ann encourages me to think of something, even if it is small, to mark the one-year anniversary. I tell her I cannot let go of his urn, cannot even walk into the storage room in my parents' place where his things are kept.

No, she says. *I don't mean his death. I mean mark the one year of your survival.*

I sit back in my chair. The "I" that I was before Kurtis died, that woman is gone. I miss her wifehood, her decisiveness, her laugh, her mental clarity, her gift for multitasking, but I am weary too of the baseless hope that she might come back. The woman I was in the Before is, I suspect, permanently lost.

If I have completely changed, I say. *Does that really mean I have survived?*

Ann asks if I truly think grief has altered everything about me.

Yes, I say, and then, *No.*

145

From the boat, we all talk about the cliffs' stone surfaces gleaming in the sunlight. We guess their height. Christopher does not want to jump. The others hesitate too. I ask the one guy who does want to leap if he thinks the climb up will be easy.

Super, he says.

I turn away from him for a moment, consider again the imposing stretch of the cliffs. When I look back, the guy is watching me.

I will if you will, he says.

At night in Mara, I am too cold and then I am too hot. A train runs through my restless sleep. The lonely blare of the horn. Of course, I know it is me that is lonely.

In the Bible, Naomi claims the name Mara as an expression of grief after the deaths of her husband and sons. The root of the name Mara is the Hebrew word for bitter. Yet, despite Naomi's declaration, she remains known as Naomi. I wonder if this is a failure of those around her to bear witness to the magnitude of her grief.

Or maybe, it is her fault. Maybe she only cries when she is alone. Maybe she keeps answering to her name like it is still hers.

I follow the guy who wants to jump more than fifteen feet up the shale, which is slick, worn to a high polish. I climb in bare feet, wearing only my swimsuit. The ascent is difficult. I focus on keeping my grip on the rocks.

At the summit, sharp grass grows in sparse patches. There is a light wind. Something grazes my feet, so I look downward. A trace of blood streaks my big toe. I slipped on the scramble to the top but I did not feel any pain. I realize I have torn four deep, parallel gashes into the skin beside my right knee. The flesh is ragged and raw.

I join the guy at the edge of the shale rock face. Christopher and the others in the boat are much farther below than I imagined. Large boulders are visible in the water at the base of the cliff.

I do not know how strong my legs—how deep the water—how far out the rocks—I have never jumped from a cliff before. I have no idea if I am going to make it. There is no being ready. Shale falls to dust at the edges.

When she asks, I tell Ann the parts of myself that have not been changed by grief are the parts I still do not know how to live with.

Grief took everything but the cockroaches, I tell her.

What are the roaches? she asks.

The intensity, I say. *The dread, the loneliness.*

I do not tell Ann or anyone that I have found Kurtis's list—the one he wrote for therapy, the things about me that bothered him. I find it because I am going through his notes on his tablet, looking for the message he sent to the guys after his bachelor party. I read his therapy list even though he would not have wanted me to. It is only five things long. One of the things *is* that I am petty.

149

You first or me?

The guy asks as we gaze across the water. He is essentially a stranger; one of Kurtis's friends I met only once before, in passing. I do not want to admit to him how afraid I am. My pulse pounds, thick in my ears.

You, I say.

He grins. When he leaps, he does so without any hesitation. I watch the gleam of the water as it flies upward, his body plunging downward. Then, a faint ripple as the dark pinprick of his head surfaces. His success does not lessen any of my fear. I watch the shadow of his body in the water. He is not swimming back to the boat. He appears to be waiting.

If you jump, I jump, I say to myself.

The fall is sustained enough that I have time to think. Afraid to live, afraid to die, afraid of how much there is to fear: it all rushes through my body.

Once I strike the lake, it is as green on the inside as it is from the outside. It rushes up my nose and burns. For a moment, I hold myself under, refusing to surface.

When I finally break above the water, the guy cheers.

I didn't think you were going to do it, he says. *It's high*.

Well, I say, pulling my wet hair out of my face. *We did it together*.

We look at each other and laugh. This is the first time I really laugh since Kurtis has died. It is not my old laugh, but a new one.

150

After his bachelor party, Kurtis tells me he has never laughed so much in his life. He has such a symphonic laugh. He throws his whole head back, his lungs capture air in a way unique to him. His entire jaw opens wide as the escalating sound piles upward. It is infectious, dirty good.

Night shrouds the lake by the time we return from boating. We all crowd around the bright crown of the fire. Once they are drunk enough, the guys shuck off their shoes and then all their clothes. They run pell-mell out of the porch's light and into the shadows cast by the weeping willows. Down by the dark iris of the lake, I just glimpse the stalks of their bodies beneath the dock lights. I can hear them perfectly though. On the water of Mara, sound carries itself a long way.

I watch as one guy spreads his arms and legs outward. He falls flat onto his stomach into the water. The sharp slap of his body striking the surface is clear and resonant. The other guys howl.

I can almost hear it. The way Kurtis's laugh would have travelled the length of the lake. I feel his laugh in every part of my body, every part I did and did not know could ache.

MoMA contracts persistent diarrhea. She is barely six months old. I worry about her constantly. I read online about all the terrible things that could be wrong with her.

She's fine, my mother assures me, rightly pointing out MoMA's enthusiasm for eating, walking, and playing has not dimmed in the slightest.

Kurtis was fine, I say. *But he died.*

My mother flinches. I put my hand over my mouth. I have spoken without thinking. I am exposed, having unwittingly revealed my distrust of life, my fear of its fragility, which I now see everywhere, though I try not to admit this to others.

That night, in my parents' guest bed, I cannot sleep again. I stare at the ceiling where a white moth is trapped. For hours, I consider the flap and slap of its pale wings against the ceiling I painted like a faux sky when I was in my early teens. It has been well over six weeks since I decided I cannot live in the apartment. Soon, I know it is time for me to move.

Maybe parenthood will make me chill, I tell him one evening.

He is mincing garlic, I am watching the water for noodles boil in its silver pot.

Amy, he says, looking at me.

It might! I say. *I've heard it changes everything about you.*

He laughs so hard it hurts my feelings.

152

Kurtis and I share a digital pinboard named Home. In it, we save ideas for our future house, which Kurtis wants to design.

Just after the one year, I log in to this board. I realize he has been adding photos to it for a long time; the board has well over a hundred pins. I have only contributed a few ideas, ages ago. All along, he was envisioning our future.

I am looking at the pinboard because I am preparing to find a new place to live. Pain howls through me, gale force.

I'm exhausted, I say to grief counsellor Ann. *Grief takes everything.*

Ann's black kitten prowls in the background of the video call. She has adopted a cat even though she is a dog person. We are talking about the ways my life has changed since he died.

You know, she says, *a lot of people I work with report that they don't like how they got there, but, after a while, they like who they are in grief more than who they were before.*

I watch the kitten tip over a water glass with one small paw.

Those people married again, I say. *They definitely have kids. They got the things they longed for.*

Ann does not argue with me. She tells me it is good I went in his place to Mara.

You are carrying him forward with you, she says.

153

I lie in bed at night scrolling the entries on a widows' board. One woman has just posted. She is in
her seventies. She writes about her first husband
who died more than forty years ago. She has been
re-married a few times since but she shares how
there is always and still a deep and tender part of
her heart that holds her first husband closely. She
says she is one of the only people still living that
remembers him. She details his favorite food, tur-
key dinner, his easy manner with children, the
way he called getting into bed "opening the mail."
She writes:

> I miss him. He was always my favorite, even
> though I loved my other husbands too.

She adds that his big feet were always warm.

You're my favorite, I say to Kurtis every night before
sleep.
  You're mine, he says.

I see another psychiatrist. His job is to assess when I might begin my return to teaching. We meet once on a video call for less than an hour. He keeps asking about my *stressful event*.

When did your stressful event occur?

What was the nature of your stressful event?

He asks so many more questions about my *stressful event* that I finally have to say something. I tell him losing your job is stressful, and so is a breakup, or a fractured ankle, or your parent being hospitalized, but your husband dropping dead and then almost dying yourself is not merely a *stressful event*. Despite me saying all of this, he continues to use the term.

He asks if my *stressful event* isolates me from my friends and family. I shake my head.

Is that so? he says in obvious surprise.

The question seems rhetorical so I do not respond. I am trying to be polite, to remain open to this stranger who seems to care more about his clipboard than he does about me.

I am a person, not a case number, I think, but do not speak out loud.

The psychiatrist asks about my writing.

Do you find it a fulfilling hobby? he asks.

Earlier in the session, I told the psychiatrist I was recently signed by a literary agent, who read the only story I have ever published. I explained this was a significant step in my career as a writer.

What's a hobby? I say. *I only have work.*

He asks if I would consider myself to have a *sarcastic sense of humor.*

No, I say.

He does not smile. I do not smile.

Once, Kurtis returns from a work trip and immediately pushes me up against the wall of our cramped living room.

I can't wait, he says.

I say his name. It sounds like the only cardinal direction I know.

156

Later, when the psychiatrist sends his report to my insurance adjustor, I receive a copy too. In it, he states that I appear cold and aloof. He writes that I likely have a propensity to make others around me feel uncomfortable and uneasy. He refers to my writing as an "engaging pastime." He notes that my hair and makeup is done. His recommendation is that I return to teaching as soon as possible.

I told you I wasn't lovable, I tell RJ.

It is my core fear and now a psychiatrist has put it in writing.

Kurtis loved you, RJ says.

I should not have let him go on that run without me. I should have been there.

It takes a month to pack up the apartment. Boxes and tape, boxes and tape, MoMA chewing on both. I take her out to pee one afternoon. Lightning has been flashing in the clouds for an hour, thunder rumbling consistently. There is a roll of thunder so long even the kids playing in the park across the road stop what they are doing and look upward.

MoMA is unbothered by the sound. She sniffs at sticks, eats grass, decapitates little purple flowers. I do not know if the blooms are poisonous so I take them from her and toss them onto the street. She tries to eat rocks, but I fish these out from her mouth, even though she tries to lock her jaw and hide the stones beneath her tongue.

A few hours later, when the rain finally falls, MoMA is making small whining noises in her sleep. I am thinking that I would like to be less afraid. Rain has long since washed the flower heads from the road. Rivulets form on the window and run continuously.

My vascular surgeon clears me for the physical labor of teaching. He tells me I need to wear a thigh-high compression stocking on my left leg when I am on my feet for hours. He warns me in three to five years, if I do not wear the stocking, my veins may permanently weaken.

Your leg seems better now, he says. *But in three years, it might balloon and never go back down. This is a real risk when you have had a clotting event as severe as yours.*

He cautions that if I get pregnant, the stent in my body will almost certainly close, provoking another deep vein thrombosis. I tell him I do not have to worry about pregnancy or pregnancy-induced clots.

I am not trying to live that long, I say to the surgeon.

Kurtis never lets us stay angry, but he always leaves physical things broken. The drawer in his bedside table that does not open. His winter tires on all year. The latch on his guitar case. He never seems to mind.

When are you going to fix this? I pester him.

Before, I wanted to make sure everything would last. Now I do not wear the stocking.

159

Katie and I go out for lunch. She wears her dark-blond hair in a thick plait. I wear my biggest pair of black sunglasses. We sit outside at a wooden table. On my right, two women in their seventies are also sharing a meal, though they are mostly done with theirs—plates empty in front of them, napkins balled in their laps. One woman's phone is ringing. When she answers, I am halfway through my lemon cake. I stop eating when the woman on the phone puts one hand over her face. I turn my head when the woman begins to sob. There is a certain kind of choking inhalation, a specific pitch to the wheeze of her cry.

Someone has died, I whisper to Katie.

Katie mouths, *Is she okay?* to the crying woman's companion.

The companion tells us the woman's husband just died in hospice. Katie hands the woman on the phone a clean napkin for her tears. When she hangs up, we offer condolences. The woman nods, sniffing into the tissue, while her companion thanks us for *being so kind*.

At one point, I tell the newly widowed woman I understand part of her pain.

You're so young, she says.

The crying woman's companion shares that her own husband died six months ago.

I don't seem sad but I am, the crying woman's companion says. *I am a very sad person.*

I never doubted the woman was sad but I understand why she had to tell me. Both women ask me how Kurtis died, how I am doing now. I try to answer but panic rises through my chest, burns as acid in my throat.

I go to the bathroom where I stand, my hands braced against the small white sink. I stare at my reflection. It has been more than a year since he died. He and I were supposed to be toasting our first year together in Vancouver. Instead, I am crying in a café washroom in Calgary.

You are here because your husband is dead, I say behind my mask. *He is not coming back.*

I need to remove my face covering to wipe snot from my nose.

You are very sad, I tell myself. *You can admit it. You still are.*

The day Kurtis dies, before my father and I leave the hospital, I ask my father how long it was before he felt any space from his grief. My father's father died suddenly when my father was in his midtwenties.

Years, he says, and then after a moment, *maybe never.*

I begin my return to teaching a few days after I move into my new place. It is October, fourteen months since. I tell my mother not to worry.

You haven't lived alone before, she says.

I cannot argue. The first time I lived entirely on my own, it lasted three weeks. Then Kurtis moved in to the apartment with me.

I have not been a full-time teacher without him either.

I have never come home and not told him about the day, I say to RJ. *There has never been a time I did this job without him.*

Online, a woman adds a thread to the widows' board. She writes:

What are our options? We can't ball up and cry forever. We're not "okay" and what other people call "strength" is really just the fact that we do not have any other choice.

So many people press LIKE on her post.

I want to share this with everyone I know, someone responds.

I reply to the woman's post as well. I write:

Grief is chronic pain. When will others allow the mourning to live without expecting them to be "cured"?

Christopher stops speaking to me. He does not tell me why or that he is going to stop. I realize his silence is deliberate only after a month of messages I send him—checking in, wondering if he would like to hang out, if he remembers the way Kurtis walked: a little bow-legged, a little sprightly?—build up into a wall of unanswered blue bubbles in our text thread.

I understand Christopher's silence is intentional when I am driving, my mind turning things over. I am headed home after a long day of teaching. It has been four months since Christopher invited me to Mara Lake. I had sent another message to him a few days earlier. I asked if something was wrong. Had I done something to upset him? There is only silence in response. In the car, sadness seeps through my body, makes it feel leaden. I grip the steering wheel and try to take deep breaths.

162

I still sleep on my side of the bed. I still think of it as my side. At night, I wake, reaching for him. In the closet, his jacket, still hanging beside mine.

I post a photograph online of me grinning with Brayden. It is one of the first photos I have shared since Kurtis died, almost seventeen months ago.

It's good to see you happy again, someone writes.

This makes me so angry I delete the comment. I do not remove the photo but I think about it.

After my first weeks back in the classroom, when I come home, the new house is so quiet, for a moment I wonder if I have lost the ability to hear. I have returned to the same school, the same job teaching upper elementary. I drive the same road—named Memorial—to and from work.

I lie on my new couch and look out of the window at a new view. I can see the river. Light silvers the water's surface. I cry until it feels like my skull will split in half.

164

When I tell Selene about Christopher's sudden silence, she sighs softly. I listen to the crackle of the candle she is burning.

How awful, she finally says.

I tell her grief therapy has taught me that, while painful, these "secondary losses" are predictable parts of the grief process.

Still, I say. *Christopher is not a loss I expected.*

I ask Selene what she thinks could have happened. She shrugs lightly.

I know Selene cannot answer my question. I know Christopher's silence may continue, may be another inexplicable part of a grief I cannot escape. When she asks, I press my hand to my sternum—to show Selene where the ache remains.

It just keeps going, I say. *All the loss.*

Yes, Selene nods. *It does.*

My return to teaching is gradual. Over the course of months, I work two days at the school, then three, then more. I forget to photocopy handouts before lessons, mix up student's names. When co-workers who have not seen me since he died come into my room and say, *Hey, nice to see you again. Hope things are good!* I stare at them. This polite small talk is a form of denial I cannot stomach. Everyone on staff is aware of what has happened. They all signed a condolence card for me, so I know they know.

My husband is dead, I say. *Things are not good.*

Sometimes, I just do not answer. Silence stretches between us.

On the days I do not teach, I lie in bed until the late afternoon. I cannot think why I would get up. Everything feels hollowed out.

Nothing matters, I tell RJ.

When he asks how much I think about dying, I tell him almost every day.

While sudden and unexplained, Christopher's silence is consistent; it lengthens into three, then six, then eight months. After more than nine months, I realize I wonder less about the abrupt break in relationship but I still wonder.

Maybe it is hard to see anything Kurtis loved remaining without him. Perhaps it is easier for Christopher to continue when he does not have any reminders. When he does not have to see how much it takes to love someone. Some people just do not want to know.

I leave Christopher's number in my phone, in case he reaches out. He never does.

When Kurtis has been dead two years, it is still an impossibility. If people ask me how long it has been, I say a year because that is how it feels. My dark heart drags with me everywhere. I see him but it is never him.

Friends text me:

Hey, doing well?

I do not reply.

The depression is noticeably worse in the second year. This is something no one mentioned in grief counselling during the first year.

168

One December, Kurtis and I drive to the mountains an hour outside of Calgary. We hike toward waterfalls, named Lower and Upper. He has been here before, but I have not. I do not expect the lower falls to be frozen, a braid of blue. Surrounding us is a low, thrumming bellow. I realize the sound is the only sign that the falls are not entirely solid. Water still flows beneath the ice, falling into a basin filled with bright aquamarine water.

The ice bothers me. I think it is one way and then it is actually another. Indeed, it all bothers me; everything surrounding us—the snow; the dirt; the stones; the trees; the sun, blocked by clouds; the ice and decay—these are things I can see, yet I cannot see through. Kurtis tells me heavy snow has closed the upper paths to the rest of the falls.

Next time, he says. But there won't be enough of that.

A Friday, driving home from school. I stop at a red light. Ahead, there is just enough falling sun in the sky to streak it pink and gold. I roll my car window down. The air is pleasantly warm. I wonder, for a microsecond, if there could be something beyond the darkness of grief, something that, albeit a long way away, is solid but light—harmonic even. As the traffic light glows green, my vehicle moves forward with the rest of the traffic.

Then again, I think, this might be all there is.

170

I attend an artist residency in upstate New York. It is midsummer, not quite two years after Kurtis dies. I was supposed to be in residence during the fall of 2020 but his death and the COVID-19 pandemic delayed my attendance. When I was first accepted Kurtis immediately asked if he could come too.

Even just to visit, he said. *I want to see it with you.*

At the airport in Calgary, I need to explain what an artist residency is to the United States border agent.

You go and work in a studio, I say. *You have to apply and get accepted.*

If you're working you need a visa, the agent says. *Do you have a visa?*

I shake my head.

It's not paid, I say. *You're awarded the time and space to write. I'm going for a month.*

If you don't need a visa, you shouldn't use the word "work."

The agent's mouth and brows are drawn in confusion.

So it's school? she asks. *You're going to school to write?*

It's not school, I say. *There are no classes. I'm writing in the woods.*

There are woods here, she says. *You don't need to fly all the way to New York for those.*

We are silent for a moment.

You said you're not getting paid? the agent finally says.

No, I say. *I'm not getting paid.*

As she hands me my passport, the agent adds, *Next time, just say you're going on vacation.*

Rebecca marks every anniversary, birthday, and memorable moment with something her husband loved. She eats his favorite food, or plays his guitar, or volunteers with rescue dogs on Wednesdays. She lights candles, talks about his love of plaid shirts with his friends.

I do not do any of these things. I cannot even stand looking at the cases that hold Kurtis's guitars. I tell Rebecca I still worry I am not remembering the right way.

Yes, Rebecca says, a note of relief in her voice. *I worry I'm not doing it right either.*

I have not been near New York since Kurtis and I were there. Since he first told me he loved me.

When I arrive at the residency, a program assistant greets me. She is a fellow resident—*visual art*—as well as the appointed liaison between the residency staff and the artists.

Writer, I say, when she asks.

She shows me to my room, which is neatly decorated: blue-and-white bedspread, soft yellow rug, dark wood dresser. There is a welcome packet on the bed. I see my name and then beneath it, again, the title: WRITER. I look at the packet for a long moment.

He knew me as a writer so much sooner than I did. I still cannot quite believe the word WRITER is mine. I take a photo, because he had told me I better show him *every single thing*.

The visual artist tells me that my sleeping quarters connect to my writing studio. I leave my suitcase beside the bed and walk into a small office, which is dark. The curtains are drawn. When I open them: a dense green wilderness of trees.

Native redwoods and black oaks, the visual artist informs me. *Some are two hundred years old.*

Most of the trees are so tall, I cannot see their crowns.

Grief counsellor Ann tells me everyone must mourn with what they have. I am telling her about Rebecca's grief rituals, which I admire but cannot seem to do myself. Symbolic gestures, Ann explains, are what some people have.

People are different, she says, looking at me through the computer screen. *Others grieve with other things.*

Writing, I say.

Yes, she replies. *This is what you have.*

During the guided tour, the visual artist shows me cruiser bikes parked in neat rows outside the residency's main building.

The grounds are extensive. Many residents traverse it on bikes. The cycling path is particularly scenic but she warns me that part of the route is unpaved and unlit.

Completely dark in the evening, she explains.

She pulls a map out of her back pocket, shows me how the paving forms a small loop within a much larger one—a circle within a circle.

The visual artist also tells me walking on the paved path is perfectly fine but cycling is best anywhere the path grows fully wild or is overgrown with grass.

That reminds me, she says.

On the map, she points out where the first aid kits are located. Inside these kits are the supplies needed for dealing with tick bites. Apparently, ticks are common in this part of New York. I stare at the visual artist in horror.

If you are really worried, the artist says, *you can bike everywhere. That keeps you mostly above the insects.*

Cycling is an entirely reasonable suggestion. Still, it strikes another kind of fear in me that I keep to myself.

A heat advisory is in effect. The weather app on my phone shows upstate New York turning deep maroon on the heat index. Because my studio does not have air-conditioning, I write late into the evening, when it is cooler.

After my eyes fully blur and I can no longer see the words on my computer screen, I close my laptop, climb into bed. Before I try to sleep, I roll over, put my phone close to my ear. I play one of his voice mails on repeat.

Hey, baber, I got a new phone. I love you and I'll see you soon.

He places spunky pauses between each of the last three words.

Please come back for me, I say.

Kurtis, I say.

Echoing through the chambers of my body, his voice.

He loved to cycle. He owned two road bikes and a mountain bike and a commuter bike, all carefully maintained. An entire shelf of our closet was dedicated to his cycling jerseys, his padded bike shorts, his bike helmets, his athletic sunglasses.

The first year we are together, Kurtis buys me a seven-speed cream-colored cruiser. He imagines us biking along city paths in the summer.

The last time he and I were on bikes, I passed out, falling off the bike he had loaned me. I tell him I have been flung off almost every bike I have ever ridden. I show him the handful of scars on my body, all from bike accidents. In the most awful fall, I tumbled into the middle of a road, cars flying by in the lane next to me. He listens, nodding along. Then, he pats the cruiser's wide, cognac leather bike seat.

Maybe one day, he smiles.

My bedroom and studio grow so warm by the afternoon that the air is hot in my throat. From my studio windows, most of which are sealed shut, I watch other residents select a bike and pedal toward the outdoor pool—just past a stand of trees. Much of the path to the pool is paved, but the last part is only long grass grown brittle from the heat. Almost all the artists cycle because during my first week there, one of the music composers went walking and a tick bit him just above his ankle bone.

Sitting in my sweltering studio, I imagine the blue crystal of the pool's waters. It is a very short bike ride there. This is what the other artists have told me. I touch the scars on my knees. Everywhere, I am slick with sweat.

The residency was not originally intended for artists. It was once a family's home—a mother, a father, four children. Then, the four children died. Then, the husband too. Only the woman remained, a wife no longer, a mother no longer.

After their children's deaths, the woman and her husband decide that the estate will become a space for artists, but it is the woman—without her children, without her husband—who sets this intention in motion.

By the time the first artists-in-residence arrive on the estate, the woman is dead too.

On my first lap of the paved path, I wobble on the bike. I have not secured the seat properly. It swings back and forth, torquing my body. I also do not understand at first that braking requires pedaling backward. As the bike glides down a slope, the slight increase in speed startles me. My hands squeeze the handlebars, searching for brake levers that are not there.

To try to manage my fear, I say to myself: *Kurtis is biking. Kurtis is biking.*

He is the one who knows how. Who holds his balance even when he shuts his eyes. Even when he flings his arms wide.

Because of all the death in the estate's history, there is the belief that the woman haunts the estate. Some artists leave offerings on the woman's grave—which is on the residency grounds—as a way of keeping peace with her spirit.

I neither visit the woman's grave nor leave a token for her. This is not out of disrespect or fear or even a disbelief in haunting. It is simply because I want my door open to the dead. Every day, every night, I wait. I wait for him to visit me.

Eventually, I feel steady enough to slowly cycle the paved loop. It winds through thick stands of trees, along the edge of a pond skimmed with algae.

When I encounter the point where the path splits, I pedal in reverse and shudder to a halt. The unpaved way is rocky. Sharp grey stones jut out from wild grass patches. So many trees line the worn trail that the canopy overhead casts complete shade. I look at the loose stones. It is uncertain terrain.

I decide to stay on the smooth path, in the sun. As I cycle back toward my room, I glide past a studio designed for visual artists or music composers. It is one of the newest buildings on the property, all knurled wood and coppery metal. The roof is a single black slope angled in only one direction. Its edge forms a dark line ascending to a single acute point.

I pay attention because of him.

During an early hour of the morning, when it is neither night nor day, a bat gets caught in the hallway outside my writing studio; an unscreened window was left open. I hear it before I see it. The bat's dark wings make a rushing noise. The creature dips and weaves through the air while I yelp, dodging its blurry movements.

This way, I keep saying, waving my arms toward the still-open window. *It's this way.*

My efforts do nothing to calm the bat, which is frantic with fear. Eventually, the bat finds its own path to the window and flies into the blue-black sky, its shape a dark form against the trees and the stars and the wide-open expanse.

183

I move a white stand fan into my room. I plug it into the outlet during the evenings, when I am finished writing. It hums loudly and one blade is crooked. The noise is too intense to sleep through and while the fan circulates the air, it does not cool the room at all. Yet, it is still something for the heat. I lie on the bed and let the breeze roll over my body.

There have been so many things he would have wanted me to tell him. The moments when he would have known joy are the most harrowing for me. He would have laughed when I mentioned trying to talk to the bat. I would have called it *pulling a National Geographic*, and he would have laughed.

I cannot believe how much pain we are asked to bear when we are alive. How, even if there is a way, no one can show us how to live with it.

One particularly warm night, I leave my room. Go
for a bike. The stars arrange themselves, clear and
vivid. I cycle the path slowly, relieved to be outside
where it is cooler. It is near the end of my time at
the residency. Light wind ripples my hair. Thin
black lampposts light the way, until they do not. I
find myself slowing to a stop at the turn onto the
unpaved path. It is the last part of the loop left to
explore. The only part of the grounds I have not yet
seen. Looking into the dark wild, I take a long,
deep breath. The night is almost opaque. Outlines
of tree trunks, spikes of stones, flickering fireflies,
all barely visible. It is true he would have seen everything he could. He loved the scenic route, the
long way around. So, I push the bicycle back into
motion. As the wheels move away from the pavement and onto the gravel, the bike sways before it
steadies. My hands shake on the handlebars, the
fenders rattling over the rough.

I look for my shadow but I cannot see it because it
is everywhere. Despite this total dark, the earth
still holds sun. Heat beads sweat at the nape of my

neck. Stones glance off the frame of the bicycle. Pushing my feet hard against the pedals, I let the bike fly blind. I listen to leaves, rustling far above me. The trees are such endless distances. Shadows shift in the brush. What might be wind. What might be breath. What is already gone.

ACKNOWLEDGEMENTS

I keep turning to tell him. I want him to know Katherine Fausset, Bridie Loverro, Zibby Owens, and the tireless teams at Zibby Books and Curtis Brown—you made this book real.

I want to spin his beam and gleam toward Shira Erlichman, Michael Goetzman, Jared Jackson, and Kimberly Kruge—my keen readers, my dear friends.

I want him to sling an arm around me, around my other beloveds: Alan and Jane Lin, Lisa and Luke Goretsky, David and Helen Vitler, Jarel Bremness, and all my extended family—how your love continues me. I want him to bring close Kathleen Byers, Nicole Dyck, Kim Everingham, Rebecca Gilbertson, Randy Johnson, Brayden Scott, Taryn Tilton, and the Thieves—you steady my shaking hands.

I want him to know. To hold him, look him in the eyes, and tell him: *Kurtis Lindsay Rei Nishiyama, you were right. Love is longer than time.*

ABOUT THE AUTHOR

AMY LIN is a writer and educator who lives in Calgary, Canada. Her work has been published in *Ploughshares* and she has been awarded residencies from Yaddo and Casa Comala.

www.amydawnlin.com

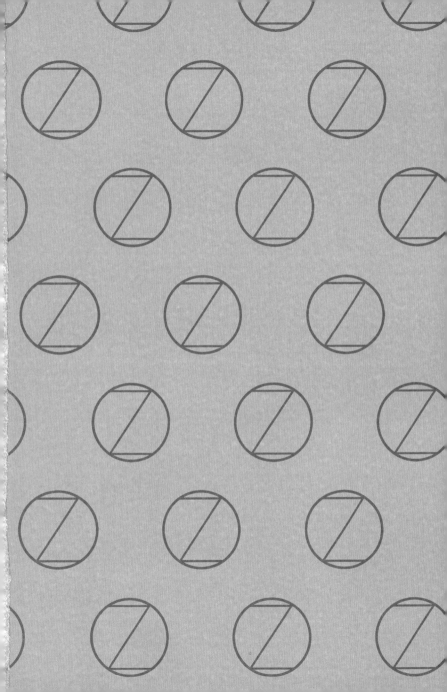

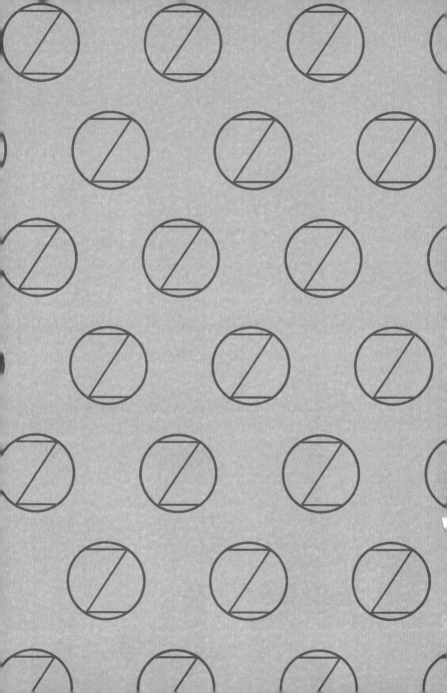